UNEXPECTED

Japan

UNEXPECTED

Japan

WHY AMERICAN BUSINESS SHOULD RETURN TO ITS OWN TRADITIONAL VALUES–AND NOT IMITATE THE JAPANESE

DONALD R. RICCOMINI & PHILIP M. ROSENZWEIG

Walker and Company
New York

First published in the United States of America in 1985 by the Walker Publishing Company, Inc.

Published simultaneously in Canada by John Wiley & Sons Canada, Limited, Rexdale, Ontario.

Library of Congress Cataloging in Publication Data

Riccomini, Donald R., 1952–
  Unexpected Japan.

  Bibliography: p.
  Includes index.
    1. Management—Japan-Miscellanea. 2. Management—United States—Miscellanea. 3. Japan-Social life and customs—Miscellanea. I. Rosenzweig, Philip M., 1955– . II. Title.
HD70.J3R53 1985   658′.00952   85–7313
ISBN 0-8027-0858-7

Printed in the United States of America

10 9 8 7 6 5 4 3 2 1

Acknowledgments

The authors would like to thank Ruth Cavin of Walker and Company for her assistance in editing and preparing the manuscript for publication; James F. Horner and Richard Dohemann of the Hewlett-Packard Company for reviewing the manuscript for the accuracy with which it depicts Japan; and Milton Friedman for reading and commenting on the manuscript.

The authors would also like to thank the following publishers for permission to quote: Houghton Mifflin, *Selections From Ralph Waldo Emerson. An Organic Anthology*, edited by Stephen Whicher (Boston, 1957); Bantam Books, *The Book of Five Rings*, by Miyamoto Mushashi (New York, 1982).

The lines quoted on page 88 are from "The Wasteland," by T.S. Eliot, from *Collected Poems 1909–1962* by T.S. Eliot, copyright © 1935, 1936 by Harcourt Brace Jovanovich, Inc.; copyright © 1964 by T.S. Eliot. Reprinted by permission of the publisher.

Preface

This book began as a reaction against the flood of articles, books, and television programs idolizing Japanese business and economic practice. As employees of a large American electronics firm, we were interested in improving productivity. We did see some good in the Japanese way—attention to detail, an orientation toward customer satisfaction, and an overriding conscientiousness. Certainly, we felt, American business could learn from Japan in these respects.

What disturbed us, however, was the tendency to romanticize the Japanese system, and to assume that whatever worked there could work here. Rarely did we hear anyone criticize the Japanese. And whatever dissent existed sometimes bordered on racism.

Uncomfortable with both the romantic and racist views, we decided to study Japanese business practices on our own. But unlike many economists who limit themselves to statistics as the main measure of a country's wealth, we also sought to understand Japanese culture, language, and customs. We wanted a comprehensive, concrete picture of what it was like to live and work in Japan. Just how, in everyday terms, did the Japanese benefit from their economic miracle? How well did they live? By trying to answer these questions—by studying Japanese schools, factories, home life, recreation, and behavior—we arrived at the fundamental premise of our book: namely, that economy and culture cannot be treated in isolation from each other. Indeed, they are inextricably linked.

Since statistics and generalities cannot communicate the reality of living and working in Japan, we decided to present our material in a more immediate and concrete way. We decided that the most effective method of presentation was as a fable— that is, as a story designed to illustrate a set of ideas. Fables deal with established facts, but in terms of a fictional narrative. They take things that are known to be true and combine them into a dramatic sequence of events. The advantage is that the reader is not just told about something—but is shown it as well. Unlike statistics or logical argument, which are by necessity abstract, fabular imagery gives us a full, vivid picture of reality.

And unlike a novel, which attempts to present characters in their full psychological complexity, a fable uses characters to represent single ideas or particular points of view. Fabular characters, therefore, are intentionally flat and one-dimensional. They are governed not by the logic of life, but the logic of argument. The hero of *Unexpected Japan*, Christopher Newman, possesses greater psychological complexity than the other characters because he grows in knowledge. Modeled on Voltaire's Candide, he is in the ancient tradition of fabular or allegorical naifs, both earnest and honest, so that although he is anxious to conform to corporate doctrine, he is also incapable of shutting out the realities of life in Japan. Newman thereby functions as a lens through which the reader can view the Japanese economic and cultural experience.

The facts presented in *Unexpected Japan* are not new, but neither are they widely acknowledged. Indeed, our research indicates that American corporate management still holds a naive view of the Japanese, and often communicates it uncritically to its employees. *Unexpected Japan*, therefore, should be of interest to anyone who would like a balanced understanding of the Japanese economy and culture—the blue collar worker, the professional, the manager, and the executive. And if the reader comes to see that culture is a strong, often pivotal determinative of economic systems, and that for this reason imitating the Japanese is not as simple or as desirable as it sounds, the book will have succeeded.

Don Riccomini
Phil Rosenzweig

UNEXPECTED

Japan

Chapter 1

Christopher Newman didn't know it yet, but he was a man with a mission.

As the limousine glided away from the curb, he set his brief-case down and glanced at his reflection in the first-floor windows. Carefully he adjusted his tie and smoothed his hair. He was always properly dressed, and often in the same way: three-piece suit, gray or blue pinstriped, white or light blue shirt, and a modest tie, asserted with a simple pin.

Satisfied that he was looking his best, Christopher grabbed his briefcase, approached the skyscraper's entrance, and stepped on the rubber mat. The automatic doors swung open, and he took the elevator to the executive offices.

"I have a ten o'clock meeting with Mr. Ridgeman," he said to the receptionist. "My name is Christopher Newman."

"Mr. Ridgeman will be with you shortly," she said, smiling. "Please have a seat."

Surveying the lobby of the executive suite, Christopher chose a seat in the corner and began to leaf through a magazine. Suddenly he was startled by a gruff voice coming through the wall of the president's office.

"Look at that! How can you justify this kind of performance?"

"Well, we've had some unexpected problems this year," said another voice. It belonged to the president of the Covenant Corporation, Franklin Ridgeman.

"Problems? Everybody's got problems, Ridgeman. But what you've got is a disaster! Two quarters without growth is unacceptable!"

Christopher looked around the lobby. The receptionist went silently about her work. Apparently no one else could hear the conversation.

"Now listen," the gruff voice continued, "if you can't turn this company around you're through! Is that clear? You'd better straighten things out in a hurry."

"We'll do our best, Mr. Lynch," said Ridgeman.

Christopher stiffened. Lynch was Covenant's chairman of the board.

"I have plans to improve our productivity," Ridgeman added quickly. "I'm confident we can turn things around."

"I don't want plans," Lynch retorted. "I want results."

A moment later the door burst open and the chairman strode from the office, walking quickly to the elevator on the far side of the lobby. He was dressed in black, with a white shirt and gold-rimmed glasses. Beads of sweat glistened on his temples and forehead. His usually pale face was suffused with red.

A secretary slipped into Ridgeman's office, closing the door behind her. Christopher sank back into his seat. He had been summoned to see the president, but he hadn't been told why. He hoped he might be in line for a promotion. Now he didn't know what to think.

After a brief pause, the secretary opened the door. "Mr. Newman, Mr. Ridgeman will see you now."

Christopher put the magazine back and picked up his briefcase. His palms felt moist as he walked into the office of the president.

"Good morning, Mr. Newman," Ridgeman said, rising from his desk. "Please, come in and take a seat."

He motioned toward a leather chair. Ridgeman was a tall, imposing man with craggy features, a steel-gray crew cut, and an air of authority.

"Mrs. Bloom," he said to his secretary, "please ask Lagrange and Merriweather to join us. Tell them Newman's here."

"Certainly, sir," said Mrs. Bloom, disappearing into the anteroom.

Despite Ridgeman's equanimity, signs of the heated conversation with Lynch were apparent. His face was somewhat pale, and his hands trembled as he reached for his chair. Pretending not to notice, Christopher forced a smile and sat down.

"I've heard good things about you," Ridgeman began, his voice still quavering slightly, "and I know the Computer Division has been pleased with your performance as a financial analyst. But now, uh, I have other plans for you. Let me tell you what I have in mind."

The shakiness in Ridgeman's voice disappeared as he warmed to his subject.

"Newman, the Covenant Corporation has had a rough time in the last few years. We've been badly hurt by foreign competition. To be specific, our Steel, Electronics, and Telecommunications Divisions have all been under intense pressure from the Japanese."

"Yes," Christopher agreed. "The Japanese are very strong."

"We're not alone, of course," Ridgeman continued. "Lots of American firms have been hurt by foreign competition. But the Covenant Corporation is going to bounce back. It's going to bounce back because our jobs depend on it."

There was a sudden knock on the door and two men entered. One wore a blue suit and had dark, deep-set eyes. The other wore a beige leisure suit and a pleasant expression. The man in blue walked over to Christopher and extended his hand.

"Hello, Newman," he said roughly. "Bob Lagrange, Vice President of Manufacturing. Heard lots about you."

Before Christopher could reply, Lagrange grabbed his hand, shook it strenuously, dropped it, and then stepped over to the wet bar in the corner of the office.

"Anyone want a drink? How about you, Newman?"

Christopher shook his head. "No, thanks."

The second man approached Christopher and smiled warmly. "I'm Morton Merriweather, Director of Personnel. Call me Mort, okay?"

Merriweather turned toward Lagrange, who was downing a drink.

"How about some orange juice, Bob?" Merriweather asked.

"Sure," Lagrange replied, swallowing. "Help yourself."

Ridgeman cleared his throat and stood up.

"Newman," he began, walking around his desk and looking straight at Christopher, "I've got an important position for you to fill. I'm going to name you Director of Corporate Productivity, and you'll report directly to me. We have to find ways to catch the Japanese, and I'm depending on you. How does that sound?"

"That, uh, well, it sounds fine," Christopher stammered. He was overwhelmed. "I'm flattered by your offer, sir, but I don't know much about the Japanese—just what I've read in a few books."

"Don't worry," Ridgeman replied. "You know business, don't you? And business is the same the world over. You'll pick up what you need to know about the Japanese. What we're interested in is how they got so strong economically. It isn't just due to dumb luck. And it isn't due to cheap energy, or natural resources either, because they haven't got any. So it must be something else. But what? What gives them the edge? That's the question. So I want you to go to Japan and see how they operate. Learn what makes them tick. Find out their secret. Then, when you've got the answer, come back and share it with us."

"Well, I'll certainly do my best, sir," Christopher said, hoping his nervousness didn't show. "When do I leave?"

"The day after tomorrow," Ridgeman replied. "Time is of the essence. I want you to learn everything about Japanese business, so I'm sending you there for a week. You'll be hosted by one of our trading partners during your stay in Japan, so you should have plenty of time."

Ridgeman paused, then turned to Lagrange and Merriweather.

"Anything you wish to add, gentlemen?"

Second drink in hand, Lagrange turned to Christopher. "Newman, there's one way to succeed in business, and that's through efficient manufacturing. The Japanese are the most efficient workers in the world. But why? What's their secret? It must be a matter of technique, Newman. They've got it, we need it, and we're going to get it. Am I right?"

"Well, I'm sure we can learn a lot from them," Christopher replied.

Lagrange smiled. He turned and made his way back to the bar.

"Anything else?" Ridgeman asked.

"One more thing," Merriweather said, smiling at Christopher. "Now, Chris, as I'm sure Bob will agree, it's people who make productivity possible. I think you should try to find out why Japanese workers are so motivated. I'm sure that Americans would be glad to learn from the Japanese. Can you do that, Chris? Can you find out how they motivate their workers?"

"I'll certainly try," Christopher answered.

"Sure, I know you will, Chris," said Merriweather. "And I know you'll succeed."

Christopher exhaled slowly and glanced around the room. It had all happened so quickly. Could he handle it? he wondered. He didn't know much about Japan, and that might be a problem. Still, as Ridgeman reminded him, he did know business, and this was a business problem. So there had to be a business solution. And besides, how hard could it be to observe Japanese techniques and apply them in the United States? He felt his confidence returning.

"I'll do everything I can to find the secret to Japanese success," he said, standing up and extending his hand to Ridgeman. "I'm sure we'll learn a lot from them."

"That's what I like to hear," said Ridgeman, accepting the

handshake. "Your new office is right down the hall. You can begin preparing for your trip as you see fit."

"Thank you," Christopher said.

"Go get 'em," said Merriweather.

"Find the secret," growled Lagrange.

Christopher nodded, picked up his briefcase, and made his way out of the room.

Christopher spent the next two days busily preparing for his trip. He rather liked his new office. Located on the forty-fifth floor, it was handsomely decorated, with fine furniture, a plush blue carpet, a solid oak desk, and matching shelves and cabinets. Across from the desk were a Sony video recorder and TV screen.

On the afternoon of his flight he watched an NBC documentary entitled "If Japan Can, Why Can't We?" As the program ended, he heard a knock on the door.

"Come in," said Christopher, a bit puzzled. It was late in the day for a visitor.

A stranger opened the door and stepped inside. He was a young man about Christopher's age, dressed casually in slacks and a corduroy jacket.

"Hello," said Christopher. "Can I help you?"

"Hi, I'm Mark Truitt," the stranger answered.

"Yes?" Christopher replied, still puzzled. "Which department do you work in, Mark?"

Truitt smiled.

"Well, I don't work here anymore. I just came by to pick up my final paycheck."

"Oh?" Christopher cleared his throat.

"Yes. You see, I used to be Director of Productivity. I guess you're my replacement."

"What?" Christopher motioned for Truitt to close the door and sit down. "What happened?"

"Ridgeman wanted to send me to Japan to learn the secrets of Japanese management. I told him it was a futile project, that we can't imitate Japan. Ridgeman got angry and demoted me, so I quit."

Truitt eyed Christopher closely, then smiled.

"They're sending you, aren't they?"

Christopher nodded. "But I don't agree with you. I think we can learn a lot from the Japanese. How else can we become as successful as they are?"

"Do you really think you'll find the answers by going to Japan?" Truitt asked. He seemed genuinely interested in what Christopher thought.

Christopher looked down at his desk. He felt vaguely uneasy—something in Truitt's confidence bothered him.

"Yes . . . yes, I do," he answered. Truitt said nothing, and Christopher's discomfort persisted.

"Are you familiar with Japanese culture?" Truitt asked. "Do you know much about their history?"

"That's not the point," Christopher replied. "We're interested in economic and business issues."

Truitt paused. "Well, I guess that makes sense," he said. His expression brightened. "Look," he said in a conciliatory tone, "I came by to wish you luck, and to offer you a small gift—something to take to Japan with you."

For the first time, Christopher noticed that Truitt was holding a package.

"Here," Mark said, handing it to him. "I hope your trip is truly educational."

"Well, thank you," said Christopher, surprised. He weighed the package in his hand momentarily, then placed it in his briefcase.

"What are your plans now?" Christopher asked. He felt more relaxed. Maybe Truitt wasn't such a bad guy after all.

"I decided it was time to make a move, so I resigned. I wasn't getting anywhere here . . . no one would listen."

"What were you trying to tell them?" Christopher asked, his curiosity piqued.

"Only that things are more complex than they appear. That history is a better teacher than computer models."

"History?" Christopher repeated.

"My degree is in history. I'm returning to the university to teach. It's less money, but what does a man—or a people—really need, anyway?"

Truitt gave Christopher a knowing look as he finished.

"Well, what I need is the secret of Japanese productivity," Christopher said, forcing a joke.

"And I hope you find it," said Mark. "Look me up when you get back, will you? I'd like to know what you learned in Japan."

Truitt wrote his address on a scratch pad.

"Okay," Christopher answered. "I'll do that. And thanks for the gift."

"Don't mention it," said Truitt. He smiled and closed the office door behind him.

Christopher put his notes into the briefcase alongside the package. "Open in Japan only" the wrapper read. Leaning back in his chair, Christopher pondered what Mark Truitt had told him. Japanese economic success was a matter of management, a question of technique. Hadn't Ridgeman and Lagrange said as much? And anyone could learn a technique if he wanted to. That was the key. Using Japan as its model, the Covenant Corporation could turn things around. There's no question, Christopher thought. We can do it.

Leaning forward in his chair, he phoned home one last time to say good-bye to his wife and daughter, then cleaned off his desk. Mrs. Bloom entered with Christopher's plane tickets, credit cards, traveler's checks, and a Japanese phrase book. He paused to say good-bye to Franklin Ridgeman, then rode a Covenant Corporation limousine to the airport. No doubt about it—this was going to be an interesting trip.

Chapter 2

Once aboard the Japan Air Lines 747, Christopher found his seat and glanced around the cabin. Most of the passengers appeared to be American executives, presumably going off to do business with the Japanese. Some were probably on their way to Tokyo for the same reason he was—to find out what made the Japanese system work. He pulled a clipboard and notepaper from his briefcase and reflected for a moment. He made a note on his pad: "American business—increased interest in learning from the Japanese."

The large plane began to taxi down the runway, and a melodic female voice came over the public address system, asking all passengers to fasten their seat belts and extinguish any cigarettes. The 747 then accelerated and lifted off the ground in one smooth movement. It banked slightly and set its course toward the northwest, in the general direction of Japan.

Christopher settled back in his chair and let out a deep sigh. The previous days had been a whirlwind of activity and preparations; at last, he was safely aboard and en route to his destination.

Soon after takeoff, the JAL cabin crew was busy passing out steaming hot towels and refreshments and providing passengers with slippers for their comfort during the long flight. Christopher watched the flight attendants closely, hoping to get an early insight into Japanese efficiency. Each of the women wore a simple black and gray kimono, and each was unfailingly polite and gentle in demeanor. They were just as courteous as Christopher had expected.

After lunch, Christopher climbed the spiral staircase to the lounge in the plane's upper level. As he approached the bar he noticed an American sitting at a small table. The man caught Christopher's eye. He smiled and waved him over vigorously. "Hey, what y'all doin'? Comin' up for a li'l ol' drink?"

As he spoke he held his glass out in front of his face and jangled the ice cubes. It was clear that he had already had a few drinks of his own.

"C'mon, take a seat," he commanded. He turned to the bartender. "Hey, you! More drink, okay?" He made motions of pouring, mixing, and drinking, to indicate what he wanted.

"Coming right up," said the bartender, smiling, and without a trace of an accent.

"Well, jus' make 'em strong," the man replied, pointing at the drinks. He picked up a glass and handed it to Christopher, who thanked him and took a seat at the table.

"I'm Henry J. Hornblower, Texas-born and Texas-bred," he said proudly, extending his hand and grinning broadly. "The 'J' is for James, but you jus' call me Hank, ya hear?"

"Sure," said Christopher, smiling and returning the handshake. Hornblower lifted his glass to toast his guest, and then took a long swallow of bourbon and branch. He wore a lime-green polyester suit and a polyester peach shirt, a Western-style string tie anchored at the neck by a large turquoise stone, and white patent leather shoes with a white vinyl belt to match. A heavy gold and stone ring adorned his pinky finger, and he wore a large cowboy hat, banded by a strip of snakeskin.

"I'm Christopher Newman," said Christopher. "I work for the Covenant Corporation."

"That so?" asked Hornblower, cocking an eyebrow. "What kind of business trip you on?"

"I'm on my way to Japan to learn how they became so successful."

"Oh, yeah?"

There was an uncomfortable silence.

"Well, if you want my opinion, those little folks can't teach us nothin'!"

"What 'little folks'?" asked Christopher.

Hornblower snorted loudly. "You know—the Japs! They can't teach us a single solitary thing! If you want to learn about business, boy, y'all come on down to Texas. Ah don't see what you 'spect to learn from the Jap'nese."

"Oh. Well, uh, why are *you* going to Japan?" asked Christopher, not quite sure what else to say.

"Ah'm going to Japan to see some manufacturing contacts about a cotton deal. Those Jap'nese want to buy some. Goin' to make shirts out of it. Ah don't like it, but they've put so many of our mills outta business Ah can't sell to no one else. Though Lord knows this Texan don't like havin' to deal with the Japs!"

Christopher was taken aback by the bitterness and resentment in Hornblower's voice. His attitude was quite different from the scholars and journalists Christopher had encountered in his reading. They had been very impressed with the Japanese; Hornblower clearly was not.

"It sounds like a good deal for you, though," Christopher pointed out.

"Oh yeah? How's that?" Hornblower demanded.

"Well, what I mean is that you get to sell them your cotton, and they make shirts and then sell them back to us. It's a fair trade, isn't it?"

"Hell, there ain't nothin' fair about it!" Hank Hornblower roared. "Are you kiddin'? It ain't free and it ain't fair! It ain't fair because we let them in free, anytime they want, and we let them sell any damn thing they please. We let them right into our markets. But it sure don't work both ways! No, sir, we can't sell free over there like they can in the U.S.A.!"

He stopped for a moment and took a long belt of bourbon, then started up again. "And one more thing—it's not just the cotton business that's bein' hurt. No, sir. It's all kinds of industries all across America—it's steel mills, and automobiles, and TVs and semiconductors and even citrus farmers. All of us is sufferin' 'cuz of the Jap'nese."

The Texan receded into his chair and called for another drink. Christopher sipped his bourbon and thought about what Hornblower had said. Japan did have protectionist laws, complex custom procedures and regulations that limited imports. Still, Christopher thought, it was hard to fault the Japanese for wanting to protect their balance of trade—after all, as an island nation with almost no natural resources, they depended on a net trade surplus for their very survival.

"Well, couldn't we work these problems out?" asked Christopher quietly. "Surely the Japanese would be willing to compromise."

"There's only one way to handle 'em," Hornblower continued, leaning across the table. "Keep 'em out! Tell 'em they can't sell here. Let 'em sell their stuff to the other slopes. Then see what happens to their 'miracle.'"

The plane pitched suddenly over some turbulence and Christopher instinctively grabbed the table for support. It leveled out and he cleared his throat for a reply.

"I don't know about protectionism," he said, half to himself. "It usually backfires, and it's isolationist. I think it's better to support a policy of free trade, and try to get everyone else to play by the same rules."

"Yeah, sure," Hornblower replied.

"Well, anyway," Christopher continued, "look at how successful the Japanese are. Look at their GNP. That's why I've been sent to study their techniques. If we can imitate the Japanese, we can be successful, too. And you can't argue with success."

Just then the bartender interrupted to tell them dinner was about to be served in the Super J Executive Class.

"Let's hope they got somethin' that sticks to the ribs," said Hornblower with a sarcastic laugh.

Christopher nodded and they made their way downstairs. "See you later, and thanks for the drink."

"Shore thing," said Hornblower. "Damn nice to talk with an American!"

Christopher walked back to his seat just in time for dinner. He ate quietly, thinking about his conversation with the Texan. Even if there was some substance to Hornblower's complaints, he thought, the anger and resentment was uncalled for. It was always better to learn than to complain.

"Excuse me," a voice interrupted suddenly. It was the passenger in the next seat.

"I'm Ernest T. Faithful," he said, extending his hand. For a moment it seemed that Christopher was staring at a younger version of himself. Faithful wore a suit and tie, vest, and wingtips. On his left hand was a new class ring. In his right hand, propped up under the light, was a copy of *The Book of Five Rings*. Faithful gave Christopher the impression he had just left school.

"Just starting out, eh?" Christopher asked the young man.

"Yes," said Ernest, looking a little embarrassed. "I just got my MBA from USC, and this is my first job. In fact, this is my first trip overseas."

"On a business trip?"

"Yes, for the Japanese-American Bank. I'm going to Japan for management training, so that I can be an enlightened manager. I've been reading this book about Bushido, the Way of the Samurai Warrior. It can really help you become a better manager, or even a better financial analyst."

"Is that so?" said Christopher, interested. "I glanced at a copy of *The Book of Five Rings* in a store, but I haven't had a chance to read it. Are there any sections that you've found especially helpful?"

"Just about all of it's helpful. It's a fascinating book that completely reveals the secret of Japanese success in business."

"No kidding," said Christopher. He noticed that the front cover of the book depicted a samurai warrior facing an American businessman, each in the same ritualistic combat pose, like mirror images of each other. The samurai held a fan over his head and extended a sword toward his opponent; the businessman curled a *Wall Street Journal* above his head and held a briefcase in his other hand. The juxtaposition struck Christopher as a little strange. One didn't normally think of an American businessman as a samurai.

"Let me read you a typical passage," Faithful continued. "This is from the first chapter:

> *It is better to wield two long swords rather than just one when facing a number of opponents alone. Also, two long swords are advantageous for taking prisoners. I need not write about such things in detail here. From one thing, know ten thousand things.*"

Christopher was puzzled. "Well, it's very interesting. I'm not sure I understand how all of this relates to business, though. It seems to have more to do with sixteenth-century samurai combat skills."

"Yes, but there's a close connection between swordfighting and management! Don't you see? Lots of this is directly applicable to management. Just listen:

> *In the path of commerce, too, there is the rhythm by which one becomes wealthy, and the rhythm by which the wealthy go bankrupt, with the difference in the rhythm according to each path. The rhythm with which things prosper and the rhythm with which things deteriorate should be understood and differentiated.*

"You see?" said Faithful. "It's a matter of understanding the rhythm. The Japanese understand the rhythm of prosperity. That's why they're so successful."

"Oh," said Christopher uncertainly. "But how does understanding rhythm help them in business? I'm not sure I see a connection."

"Well, it's all very subtle, and it takes a lot of patience to understand. The whole Japanese way is based on subtlety and patience, so we can't expect to become enlightened overnight.

Actually," said Faithful, his voice trailing off, adopting a sheepish look, "I don't really understand it myself. But I'm going to learn! It just takes time."

"Maybe so," Christopher allowed. "But I think there has to be more to it than what you've just read."

"Oh, no! I can assure you—the whole book's exactly like this. And I'll bet we could catch up to the Japanese in no time if every American manager would just study this book."

Christopher wasn't sure what to think. How could you use something correctly if you didn't understand it? Maybe the book could provide some background, but to really understand the Japanese economic miracle, you had to spend time studying their production and management techniques. His own in-depth study would probably be more useful in the end, he concluded.

"Say," Faithful continued, "do you think you could help me memorize a few lines? I'll bet I'd really impress my boss if I could recite a passage from *The Book of Five Rings* when I get to Tokyo."

"Gee, I'd like to help," Christopher replied, "but I've got some work of my own to do. Thanks for reading those passages to me, though."

As Christopher settled back into his chair, the paragraph about rhythm returned to mind. It was something he had heard before, but he couldn't quite place it. Was it from a poem he had read? Or perhaps from a folk song? Suddenly, he remembered:

> *For everything there is a season,*
> *And a time for every purpose under heaven:*
> *A time to be born, and a time to die;*
> *A time to sow, and a time to plant;*
> *A time to get, and a time to lose . . .*

It occurred to him that the Japanese emphasis on the rhythm of all things was, in the end, indistinguishable from Ecclesiastes's emphasis on time and change. It really wasn't necessary to read *The Book of Five Rings* to learn about rhythm. All you had to do was remember Ecclesiastes.

Christopher read for a few minutes, then called for a night-cap from the stewardess. Soon he dozed off, his sleep echoing faintly with the rhythm of Ecclesiastes.

Several hours later, Christopher was awakened by the gentle sound of a chime. The plane was just a half hour from Tokyo, and was beginning its final descent. As the jet turned slightly he could see, in the distance, the soft undulations of the island mountains, with the blue Pacific Ocean visible in the foreground. From this vantage point it was easy to understand why the Japanese thought of themselves as living on the island of the gods.

Again the chime rang gently. It sounded like a traditional ceremonial gong, but there was no gong to be seen. The Japanese had cleverly programmed a small computer-driven chime so that it rang and vibrated like a real gong. It was, Christopher reflected, typical of the Japanese ability to absorb new technologies while still retaining, through the technology itself, a connection with their ancient culture. That was true progress, he thought. Now every Japanese worker, by purchasing the mass-produced device, could have his own ceremonial gong.

"Hello," said a high-pitched voice behind him. It was a stewardess, smiling in a demure and deferential way. "Everything okay?"

Christopher nodded and she proceeded to the next passenger.

"Everything okay?" she asked. She spoke with the same studied politeness to each passenger. Christopher was impressed with the uniformity she managed to achieve.

As the plane descended, the mountains sharpened into jagged, barren peaks. Soon Christopher could make out Tokyo Bay and the huge Tokyo–Yokohama metropolitan area. The city gradually resolved itself into a network of lines, points, and curves; geometric shapes which, from the air, resembled two-dimensional paintings he had seen in modern art museums. Soon he could make out skyscrapers, docks, and extensive freeway systems—the image of a modern industrial city.

Christopher buckled his seat belt and prepared for the landing, putting his papers away and bringing his seat back upright. The landing was as smooth and effortless as the takeoff, and the plane taxied slowly to the gate. Christopher gathered his things, said good-bye to Faithful, and slowly made his way out of the plane. Once past customs, he tried to make himself conspicuous so that his contact could locate him.

"Mr. Newman?" a polite, accented voice said behind him.

Christopher turned around and found a smallish Japanese man standing next to him. The man smiled and bowed deeply.

"I am from Wanasumi Company. My name is Takeo Sakatumi."

"Pleased to meet you, sir," said Christopher, shifting his briefcase to his opposite hand and extending a handshake. Mr. Sakatumi shook his hand awkwardly, then reached into his coat pocket and produced a business card.

"It is customary to exchange card," he said, handing it to Christopher.

"Thanks," said Christopher. "But I'm afraid I don't have any cards with me."

Mr. Sakatumi smiled and gestured for Christopher to follow him toward the baggage claim area. He wore a tailored suit, dark gray with light pinstripes, balanced by a white shirt and black tie. He was a head shorter than Christopher, but walked with a paradoxical air that seemed to combine deference and pride.

After helping Christopher get his luggage, Mr. Sakatumi escorted him to a special parking lot for limousines.

"We have Wanasumi Company car to drive us to Tokyo," he said, motioning to an automobile with an attentive chauffeur standing alongside. The chauffeur, smartly dressed in a uniform, cap, and immaculate pair of white gloves, placed Christopher's bags in the trunk and held the car doors open for his passengers, then slid in behind the wheel and began the drive into town.

"Is it a long drive to Tokyo?" Christopher asked as the car entered the thick traffic that led from the airport into the capital.

"It will take two hours," Mr. Sakatumi answered evenly.

Christopher wondered that the airport would be so far from town until he looked out the car window at the congested freeways and the cars inching along, bumper-to-bumper. Then it was easy to see the drive could take two hours. At least it would be comfortable.

The two men rode in silence for several minutes. Feeling a bit awkward, Christopher tried to strike up a conversation with his host.

"Do you have a family?" he inquired.

"Yes, Mr. Newman. I have family."

"Please call me Chris," said Christopher with a smile, hoping to establish a friendly rapport. "Do you have any children?"

"I have son. He attends fine school, Mr. Newman."

"That's nice," said Christopher.

Mr. Sakatumi smiled and bowed his head.

They rode in silence until the Tokyo skyline came into view. Then Mr. Sakatumi reviewed Christopher's itinerary for the next day: wake-up call at six thirty; breakfast at seven fifteen, leave hotel for factory at eight, begin factory tour at eight forty-five, complete tour at eleven fifty-five, lunch at twelve, visit school at one thirty, return to hotel at four, leave for dinner at Mr. Sakatumi's home at six thirty, return to hotel at ten, sleep at ten thirty. Free time between four and six thirty.

"Wow," said Christopher, marveling at the Japanese genius for organization. "That's quite an itinerary."

"Following day begin at six thirty . . ."

"That's okay," said Christopher quickly. He was amazed at how detailed the Japanese were, even in the itinerary. Clearly the purpose was to let him see as much of the Japanese system as possible.

The chauffeur weaved his way through Tokyo's busy streets, gliding smoothly between cars and buses, trucks and pedestrians, timing streetlights almost perfectly. What impressed Christopher the most about Tokyo was that despite the crush of people, everyone and everything seemed to move in an orderly fashion. At one point, while waiting for the traffic ahead to clear, Christopher caught a glimpse of a sea of people flowing toward a tram. As the car reached capacity, uniformed men shoved the remaining passengers into the cars, then slid the doors shut, so as to use every bit of space. Christopher could see the people's faces pressed against the window glass, unable to move until they reached their destination. He felt a bit claustrophobic, and instinctively shifted in his seat, as though to remind himself that he was free to move. As the tram moved off, the space before it once again began to fill with people.

They drove to Shinjuku, a modern business and hotel district on Tokyo's west side. Christopher looked up in admiration at the tall and lean skyscrapers. They reminded him of the headquarters of the Covenant Corporation.

"Here is hotel," said Mr. Sakatumi as the car accelerated, turned, and then slowed to a stop.

"Great! Is this it?" asked Christopher, pointing to a small building.

"Oh, no. Your hotel is next door. You will stay at the Keio Plaza Hotel. What you see here is a modular hotel, for Japanese only."

They got out of the car and walked toward the modular hotel. Christopher could see a broad structure made up of cast concrete modules, each about three feet square and six feet deep, stacked one on top of another. Through the windows, Christopher could see that each module contained a sleeping mat, a sheet and blanket, a small Sony television suspended from the ceiling, and a small, built-in vanity with a mirror and a cabinet for toiletries. Most of the modules were occupied, and the movement of the patrons, as they switched television channels or smoothed their mats or blankets, reminded Christopher of a giant beehive, inhabited by hustling, bustling workers imbued with an aura of order and organization.

"Who are these people?" Christopher inquired.

"These are employees who do not want to go home for the night," replied Mr. Sakatumi. "Many family men stay here all week, to save time and money in commuting. Companies encourage this, to help fellow employees get necessary rest."

"I don't think I'd fit," said Christopher, eyeing the tiny modules closely.

"Is not for foreigners," Mr. Sakatumi assured him. "You too tall," he added, smiling. "Please, come this way."

Mr. Sakatumi escorted Christopher through the tall doors of the Keio Plaza Hotel and across the lobby to the registration desk. The hotel was luxurious, first class by any international standards. Christopher checked in, thanked Mr. Sakatumi, and rode the elevator to his room on the thirty-fifth floor.

After unpacking and calling his wife, Nancy, as he had promised, Christopher made a few notes about Japanese efficiency and organization, then turned in. It had been a long but fascinating day, and his trip had just started.

Chapter 3

On his first full day in Tokyo, Christopher awoke at 5 A.M., well before dawn. He was wide awake and couldn't get back to sleep, partly because he was still on American time, but mostly because he was excited about his mission to Japan.

He rolled out of bed and walked across the dark room to the window. Opening the curtains, he looked out toward the east. Greater Tokyo stretched out in all directions, its night lights still on, the first red rays of sunlight more than an hour away. Even in the early morning he could see a city in motion: buses taking people to work, trucks and commuter trains hurrying toward their destinations, and traffic lights flashing different colors. Viewed from the thirty-fifth floor, Tokyo was a sharp pattern of lights, some fixed and some in motion; and the city pulsated to a silent, steady, relentless rhythm.

After washing and dressing, Christopher looked over his notes and reviewed a few chapters from *Theory Z*, a book about how American business could learn from Japan. He took a clipboard and pad of paper from his briefcase and jotted down a heading for the day's notes. Across the top of the page he wrote SECRETS and underlined the word twice. Whenever a secret of Japanese productivity was revealed, he was going to be sure to write it down.

Christopher ate breakfast in the ground-floor restaurant, and at precisely 8 A.M., Mr. Sakatumi arrived to pick him up. Mr. Sakatumi bowed deeply to his guest, and they walked out of the hotel to a chauffeur-driven Wanasumi Company car idling softly in the driveway. The two men slid into the back-seat.

"How are your accommodations, Mr. Newman?" asked Mr. Sakatumi, once they had made themselves comfortable.

"Just fine, thanks," Christopher replied.

"We will visit factory this morning. We will arrive at Toshima Motor Company at eight twenty-five, and you will spend the morning touring facility. I will meet you again at eleven fifty-five and we will then have lunch together."

"Great," said Christopher. "I've been looking forward to seeing the inside of a Japanese factory for quite a while. You know, I'm a great admirer of the Japanese way."

Mr. Sakatumi smiled and bowed his head.

Christopher had read about the Toshima Motor Company, one of Japan's top motor vehicle manufacturers. Its name derived from the Toshima district in northern Tokyo where its sprawling complex of plants and offices were located. TMC, as it was known, produced a full line of compact automobiles and trucks, and had built a reputation for dependability, quality, and lasting consumer value. Its products had secured a large share of the Asian market; TMC cars and trucks were a frequent sight on roads from South Korea all the way to Indonesia. Not surprisingly, the TMC factory had become a favorite showcase of Japanese industry, and foreign visitors eagerly trooped through the facility by the dozens, hoping, like Christopher, to discover how the Japanese had become so successful.

The car turned into the TMC parking lot and pulled into a slot near the executive offices. Facing the entrance was a small Japanese rock garden, with a cluster of trees meticulously arranged amid an expanse of carefully raked pebbles. No stone was out of place. Christopher was impressed—it was a picture of Japanese grace, beauty, and order. He imagined that the factory would be every bit as wonderful.

Mr. Sakatumi introduced Christopher to his host and guide, a middle-aged TMC employee in a gray suit named Mr. Suzuki.

"It is an honor to welcome you to our modest facility, Mr. Newman," said Mr. Suzuki, bowing deeply.

"Oh, I'm really happy to be here," Christopher answered pleasantly. "I hope I can learn a lot so that the Covenant Corporation can improve its operations and be just as productive as the Japanese!"

Mr. Suzuki smiled and bowed again, and led Christopher through a pair of steel doors, down a long corridor, and into one of the main production floors. Plant #3, as it was called, resembled in its physical dimensions many factories Christopher had seen in the United States. It was a large open area, rectangular in shape and roughly the size of a football field. There were no internal walls or barriers, just a single immense room. Overhead, built into the thirty-foot ceiling, were tracks that carried partially assembled vehicles on rails, moving them effortlessly from one part of the factory to another.

The plant floor was bustling with activity—equipment was humming and pumping and whirring, and Christopher could see scores of TMC workers rushing about with great intensity and purpose. The noise level was loud, but far from overwhelming.

Christopher noticed a few obvious differences from the Covenant Corporation's factories in America. TMC's Plant #3 was tidy, in absolute order. Nothing was out of place or dirty. There was very little inventory lying around; very little aside from what was actually being built. Even more impressive were the workers, who moved quickly and efficiently. They were dressed in blue jumpsuits and black sneakers, and wore blue caps with the TMC insignia.

"Let us look at typical work station," said Mr. Suzuki, guiding Christopher to a nearby spot. "This is where rear bumper is attached to automobile body."

Christopher observed that partially completed chassis were tracked to this area by the overhead rails and then lowered to the floor. A crew of four workers moved briskly, taking bumpers and moving at a rapid clip to fit, weld, bolt, and then test each part as it was connected to the body. It was imperative that the work be done quickly since a new auto body would be delivered exactly twenty-eight seconds later.

Christopher saw that the workers were totally absorbed in their tasks and didn't even notice his presence. *Fit, weld, bolt, test; fit, weld, bolt, test*—their movements were perfectly timed to this staccato rhythm, which they responded to on a seemingly unconscious level. Taking a pencil from his coat pocket, Christopher recorded two important secrets of Japanese success: *concentration* and *coordination*.

"These men are trained specialists," Mr. Suzuki remarked.

"They're amazing," Christopher agreed. "I've never seen such skill."

"It is skill, yes; but it is practice, too. This team specializes in rear bumpers. They have worked together attaching rear bumpers for twelve years. Not long ago, after they had installed their one-millionth rear bumper, they were honored with membership to Toshima Productivity Hall of Fame. They are good because they repeat the same operation over and over."

"Impressive," said Christopher. He raised his clipboard and made note of two more secrets of Japanese productivity: *specialization* and *repetition*. He watched the team work for a few more moments, marveling at their machinelike precision, their economical movements honed by years of performing the same motions. Each man knew the other men's moves; and each repeated his own motions so exactly that the others could anticipate them. They resembled moving parts of a watch, perfectly in synch, never faltering. *Fit, weld, bolt, test.*

Christopher cleared his throat. "Uh, what's the failure rate of rear bumpers?" he asked in a serious tone.

"It is zero," answered Mr. Suzuki with scarcely a pause. "That man, with red arm-band, is the team's quality specialist. He must make certain that work is acceptable before allowing it to be sent on. In this way, quality is built into product."

"I see," said Christopher.

The Japanese host and his American guest walked along the assembly line, stopping at several other work stations. Christopher studied each one. He marveled at the silent speed of the workers, whose movements were so regular and unfailingly consistent that they were hardly distinguishable from the rest of the machinery. The entire production floor, it seemed to Christopher, was one complex piece of equipment with many interrelated parts, some made of gray metal, and some attired in blue jumpsuits. All parts moved smoothly, regularly, with a single rhythm dictated by the flow of production. It was a remarkable sight, although there was something about it that slightly troubled Christopher.

"Does TMC make much use of robotics?" Christopher asked his host.

"We use little robotics, Mr. Newman," Mr. Suzuki replied, smiling and inclining his head toward Christopher. "We do have some, of course, for such things as welding. But truth is, I believe, that too much attention is given to robotics. It is our people, and not robots, that is key to productivity."

"Well, your workers certainly are impressive," Christopher agreed.

"Oh, we have much improvements to make," Mr. Suzuki replied, a proud smile belying his modest words. "But please, these men are not 'workers'. They are members of the TMC family, and are called fellow employees."

"Do they belong to a union?"

"Of course. They are part of TMC Union. It takes care of the fellow employees and provides for all of their needs."

"Are there ever disputes between labor and management?"

"Oh, no! We all believe in 'cooperative unionism'. The union agrees with management on all matters. It is Japanese way. All parts of the TMC family must honor each other and work together. Success result from harmony."

Christopher whipped out his pencil and made another note. It's just as I had expected, he thought to himself. Japanese factories were exemplars of harmony.

The tour continued through other parts of the TMC complex. They visited Plant #1 where engines were assembled, they passed through Plant #4 where auto bodies were painted, and they watched the vibration analysis and final testing in Plant #5. Christopher saw that all operations were performed quickly, thoroughly, and exactly according to specifications. Again he sensed the rhythm: *Fit*, *weld*, *bolt*, *test*; *sand*, *prime*, *paint*, *wax*. It was just as Lagrange had told him: the production lines hummed. The flow of production never rested, but continued at a demanding and relentless pace.

"Say, Mr. Suzuki," Christopher asked. "Do these production lines ever stop? Do they ever shut down?"

"Very rarely" came the reply. "It is very rare, and very serious, to ever stop production."

"Well, how do you keep the line running all the time?"

"It is simple. We never turn it off."

"Can you explain that further?" Christopher persisted, a bit puzzled.

"Certainly. We stress complete harmony with manufacturing process. We adjust our actions to the needs of production. Since we can only produce automobiles when the process is running, we must never shut it down. It is really a very simple matter."

"I see," said Christopher, who jotted down the reply and made a note to give it further thought at a later time.

Mr. Suzuki escorted Christopher into a final part of the TMC factory, and showed him the huge presses that transform sheets of metal into contoured auto bodies. A mechanical tracking device then took hold of these molded parts and fed them one at a time into an enormous punch press. With a powerful crunch, the press stripped the excess steel from the contoured bodies and then flowed them to the next operation, where they were welded together and took the form of an automobile. Many of these operations were automated, but there were nevertheless several figures in blue jumpsuits carefully watching the process, monitoring the flows, checking for any defects.

In this plant floor, as in each of the others Christopher had visited that day, large Japanese characters appeared on each of the four walls.

"Say, what do those words mean?" Christopher asked.

"There is one character on each wall, Mr. Newman, standing for the four principles of the Toshima Motor Company. They are: Work, sweat, loyalty, order."

"Well, I guess those are appropriate words!" Christopher said in a pleasant voice, having seen plenty of each that morning. Mr. Suzuki nodded in a neutral way.

Christopher was led out of the production floor and into an adjacent building with conference rooms and a few offices. Mr. Suzuki guided his guest into a lounge with sofas and chairs, and a large tank of steaming green tea against the far wall.

"Would you like tea, Mr. Newman?" asked Mr. Suzuki as he reached for a pair of cups.

"Sure."

"You may be seated if you wish."

"Thanks. It's nice to take the weight off my feet. You know, that's quite a factory you have!"

"Thank you," said Mr. Suzuki, sipping his tea. He paused for a moment, and then turned to address Christopher. "We have completed our tour of facility. If you have any questions, I will try to answer them."

Christopher thought for a brief spell. The plant tour had been very illuminating. He had written down what he thought were the most important elements of Japanese productivity, but he decided to ask for his host's perspective as well.

"Oh, there are many reasons for our modest achievements," began Mr. Suzuki in his characteristically understated tone. "The most important, I believe, are three: Loyalty to company, lifetime employment, and our national system of education. All else follow from these things."

"I guess your workers really are loyal, aren't they?"

"Not just fellow employees you saw on the production floor, Mr. Newman, but all Japanese employees are loyal to their firms and do everything in their power to make them succeed. The managers, engineers, technicians, and everyone else at TMC show deep loyalty to company."

"How do you keep people from going out on their own?" asked Christopher.

"I beg your pardon, Mr. Newman?"

"How do you keep your most talented engineers from leaving to start up their own companies?"

"I do not understand," said Mr. Suzuki with a quizzical expression.

"Aren't some of your best engineers and managers tempted to go out on their own? You know, line up some venture capital and then go into business for themselves?"

"Oh! Now I see! But we have no such problem in Japan. Our system of lifetime employment make it unnecessary for people to leave company. We therefore have stability and continuity. And no one would leave voluntarily, for to do so would be dishonorable."

"I see," said Christopher, somewhat surprised by Mr. Suzuki's response. Stability and loyalty were fine qualities, but he wondered whether movement between firms and the founding of new companies was necessarily bad or dishonorable. That wasn't the case in America, where innovations seemed to emerge from the independent entrepreneur. He thought of William Shockley, co-inventor of the transistor, who left Bell Labs to start his own firm. Soon some of Shockley's associates, feeling constrained, left to form their own companies, each of which sought to improve and develop new applications for Shockley's invention. Shockley's labs begat Fairchild, which begat Intel, and so on in an ever-expanding spiral of growth and innovation. Scores of engineers were seeking to build a better mousetrap. For the first time, Christopher saw that such development was lacking in Japanese industry. The Japanese, it seemed, were more interested in preserving harmony and perfecting existing technologies than creating new ones. And that approach, Christopher reminded himself, had produced some pretty impressive results and had made employment in Japan highly attractive, since the employee wasn't constantly worried about layoffs. Christopher was attracted to the freedom of the American system, but admired the stability and security implied by the Japanese promise of lifetime employment.

"Please tell me a little about TMC's policy of lifetime employment," he asked, hoping to learn something that the Covenant Corporation might want to put into practice. It would be wonderful to return home with specific recommendations about Japanese practices that could be transferred immediately into the American workplace.

"It is important policy. It is wonderful example of mutual trust and harmony that exists at TMC."

"It sounds like a fine idea," Christopher agreed. "Tell me something—how do you manage to guarantee full employment during economic downturns? How does it affect TMC's profitability?"

"During slow economic times, we let go of woman employees. That helps keep costs down."

"You do what?"

"Like most large Japanese firms, Mr. Newman, TMC has a work force of semi-skilled women. They are employed when business is up, and sent home when times are not so good."

"You lay them off? But I thought you guaranteed employment for a lifetime!"

"That is partially true, Mr. Newman. By exercising flexibility with our secondary work force of women, we are able to guarantee continuing employment for men. That is how system works."

"But isn't that discrimination?" Christopher asked, a bit incredulous. It was becoming clear that TMC's employment policy would be difficult to implement at the Covenant Corporation, or almost any other American company.

"Oh, no. It is only fair. Of course we have different roles for men and women in our company. Women cannot perform jobs at the same level as men. That is well understood. You will notice, Mr. Newman, that naturally all executives at TMC are men. It is like that all over Japan. It is the Japanese way."

Christopher was surprised to hear that "harmony" and "mutual trust" seemed to include sex discrimination and unequal opportunity. He thought for a moment of his wife, who had done just as well in business school as he had, and who now held a comparable job. What would she think of a system that favored men and barred women from advancement? What would most Americans think? Mr Suzuki seemed convinced that the Japanese way was natural, inevitable. Christopher wasn't so sure.

"Any other questions?" asked Mr. Suzuki, serenely sipping his green tea.

"Not for the time being," Christopher replied. He gazed quietly across the room, a bit bewildered by Mr. Suzuki's revelations.

"I hope you have enjoyed your visit, Mr. Newman."

"It's been fine. I'm very impressed with how your factory works. It's every bit as efficient as I had imagined."

The two men stood up and walked back to the front desk, where Mr. Sakatumi greeted them with a deep bow.

"It is exactly eleven fifty-five and now time for lunch," Mr. Sakatumi announced. "Let us go to restaurant."

Christopher turned and thanked his host at the Toshima Motor Company, and followed Mr. Sakatumi out the front door. Once again, Christopher noticed the small rock garden. Its precise ordering of pebbles and perfectly shaped bonsai trees seemed a perfect complement to the meticulous ordering of men and parts on the TMC production line. Culture and technology, it appeared, were united into a seamless continuity—and all this was possible because of the traditional Japanese devotion to order and symmetry. It was, Christopher reflected, quite remarkable.

Chapter 4

After a lunch lasting precisely an hour, Mr. Sakatumi announced that their next stop would be at a special school. Christopher was quite interested because everything he had heard about the Japanese educational system was complimentary. And it was clear that education, as practiced in Japan, was a major reason for the Japanese economic miracle.

Mr. Sakatumi escorted Christopher out of the restaurant and across the street to a small building adjacent to the Toshima Motor Company complex. Constructed of large gray concrete slabs, it looked like an annex of the factory, or perhaps a public housing unit. Since this was an industrial area, and since Japanese zoning laws are extremely strict, Christopher assumed the building was an outlying part of the factory.

"Are we stopping at another TMC division before going to the school?" he asked.

"This *is* the school," said Mr. Sakatumi, gesturing toward the building.

"Gee. I'm not used to seeing a factory and school so close together. In America, we usually put schools in quiet places, near the children's homes. We try to keep them away from factories."

"Ah, this is not America," said Mr. Sakatumi, smiling. "For Japanese, study and work are the same thing. Education is our chief tool for shaping national destiny. Education increases productivity. It must prepare students to become efficient, dedicated workers. Each school has a motto to explain this. This school's motto is 'study, sweat, work.'"

Just like at the factory, thought Christopher. He noted the correlation on his clipboard.

"This is a *juku* for five-year-olds," said Mr. Sakatumi.

"Oh! A kindergarten," said Christopher, smiling as he thought of kindergartens in the United States.

"This is not a kindergarten, Mr. Newman," Mr. Sakatumi corrected. "This is a *juku*, a special preparatory school to help children study for the entrance exam for first grade."

"There are entrance exams for first grade?"

"Naturally. Enrollment at the best primary schools is very limited, and competition for admission is intense."

"Why is it so important to get into a particular primary school?" Christopher asked.

Mr. Sakatumi stopped walking and looked at Christopher. Carefully, he explained how Japanese schools worked.

"If a Japanese child does not get into an excellent primary school, Mr. Newman, he will never gain admission to the best high schools. If he does not attend a fine high school, he has no chance of entering the top universities. And only graduates from Japan's best universities can pursue well-respected careers with our best companies. So it is very natural that entrance into primary school is a most important time in a person's life. Children are sent to *jukus* to improve their chance of entrance exam success. Parents pay up to $1,000 a week for their children to attend the best *jukus*."

Christopher was a bit perplexed at this explanation. "But these are preschoolers, five-year-olds. Isn't it a bit early to start such a stiff program of study?"

Mr. Sakatumi did not answer immediately. Uncomfortable with the silence, Christopher continued. "Isn't there any concern about the pressure on the children? Couldn't it be bad for them?"

Mr. Sakatumi had lowered his eyes. He seemed embarrassed, not by the substance of Christopher's question, but by his effrontery at bringing it up.

"Parents want what is best thing for children," he said at

last, looking at Christopher with a polite smile. "It is best for children to study and get good job."

Christopher had the feeling that he had done something distasteful, violated some unspoken code of etiquette. He looked away, chagrined and feeling a bit guilty. After all, he was a guest in Japan, and Mr. Sakatumi was his host. What right did he have to question Japanese ways? And look what they had accomplished since World War Two. Starting as a war-ravaged nation with a devastated industrial base, Japan had developed into a powerful economic machine. In the same short time, the United States had lost its position of dominance, thanks to excessive government spending, short-term business decisions, emphasis on mindless consumption instead of prudent saving, and loose educational standards. So who am I to criticize? thought Christopher. After all, his mission to Japan was to help him *learn from* the Japanese, not to fault them.

As they reached the school building, Christopher noticed a group of mothers and children waiting at the entrance. Several of the mothers began calling out eagerly to Mr. Sakatumi, whom they recognized as a member of one of Japan's leading firms, and whom they had often seen escorting visitors through the school. They were all quite concerned about their children's chances for future employment, and took every opportunity to curry favor with him.

As each mother spoke she pushed her child forward, telling the child to behave, to bow more deeply, and to show greater respect to the honored visitors. Mr. Sakatumi, for his part, smiled beneficently upon the children, showing no favorites. If any child failed to behave properly or bow deeply, he was shoved into position and was told to apologize to Mr. Sakatumi, which he invariably did.

Turning to Christopher, Mr. Sakatumi remarked, "These are *kyoiku-mama*, or education mamas. They are fiercely devoted to the well-being of their children. They take them to school, wait while they are in class, take them home, and oversee their homework."

Christopher was taken aback by the mothers' pushiness but tried not to judge or criticize. "Well, they certainly show more interest in their children than American mothers," he said, looking at the positive side. "Do the mothers supervise the children's playtime, too?"

"There is little time for play," said Mr. Sakatumi in a neutral tone. "To get a job, children must study."

There was a sudden commotion at the entrance. A *kyoiku-mama* was trying to accompany her son into the classroom, a practice strictly forbidden to avoid placing excessive pressure on the child. So much determination, thought Christopher. It made him feel uneasy. He heard Mr. Sakatumi gently remonstrate the overzealous education mama. She shrank meekly back into the group.

"*Kyoiku-mama* have great love for son," Mr. Sakatumi explained. "Please excuse improper action."

Christopher nodded understandingly.

"Please to enter classroom," said Mr. Sakatumi, beckoning and smiling.

They took seats at the back of the classroom. The classroom was small, with a blackboard at the front of the room and twenty-four child-size desks precisely arranged in four neat rows. The room was clean and in perfect order. Large Japanese characters stood out on the walls: *Study*, *sweat*, *work*. Christopher made a quick note on his clipboard.

All of the students had taken their seats and waited quietly for their teacher to arrive. The children were dressed in navy-blue uniforms with the emblem of the school stitched on the blazer, and they were perfectly still and orderly as they waited.

Presently, the teacher entered the classroom and proceeded to the lectern. She was a pretty young woman with a pleasant smile. She took the roll silently and then addressed the class.

"Today the class will study Japanese history and English language," Mr. Sakatumi explained in an undertone. "Japanese history is necessary to give children loyalty, and English is the language of commerce. First, however, she will review some Japanese language lessons."

The teacher began by using a set of large flash cards with Japanese characters. She held up a card and then called on a student, who quickly spoke the name of the character aloud. Then she raised another character and called on a different youngster, who also provided the right answer. This process continued for several minutes. The teacher was pleasant but serious, and the children were alert, businesslike, and disciplined. They were also well prepared, rarely failing to identify a character properly. Christopher wondered how many times each child had reviewed this lesson under the relentless gaze of a *kyoiku-mama*.

Mr. Sakatumi leaned over toward Christopher as the drill continued.

"This is a most important part of education, Mr. Newman. Japanese children must learn two sets of characters. One set, *kana*, has forty-eight characters and is phonetic. The other set, *kanji*, comes from Chinese, and each Japanese child must learn at least 1,850 different characters by sixth grade. And a high-school graduate must know several thousand. It is a difficult task. Children must work hard to memorize them."

"Judging from the looks of it, these kids are doing pretty well," said Christopher as he watched the lesson proceed in an orderly and rhythmic fashion.

The teacher concluded the drill, and began a brief lesson on Japanese history. First, she pulled down a large map showing Japan, Korea, and most of China. The students continued to sit attentively in straight rows, posture erect, hands on desks, all eyes on the teacher. It was hard to believe that they were five years old.

With Mr. Sakatumi translating, Christopher heard the teacher tell the children about the Meiji Restoration of 1868, which marked the beginning of national modernization. She talked briefly of industrial progress and social reforms, and made mention of the Russo-Japanese War. Christopher listened closely as she broached the period of Japanese expansion.

"Now we will talk about China and Korea," the teacher said. "We will talk about the time Japan went to those countries. Yukio, can you tell us which country is China?"

A small boy in the front of the class stood and identified the country by color.

"Very good, Yukio. Emi," the teacher asked a girl in the middle of the room, "do you know which is Korea?"

Emi rose and correctly identified Korea.

"Very good. Now, class, can you tell me all at once which country is Nihon?"

The students rose simultaneously and called out that the green nation was Japan.

"Very good, class," said the teacher, smiling. She was obviously pleased. Her voice was soft and melodic and she had clearly established a rapport with the children.

"Today we learn about Japanese in China in the 1930s, long before you were born. Japan advanced into China. Sometimes Chinese people died but many Japanese died, too. It was a sad time for all. Now there is much happiness between Japan and China.

"In 1910 Japan went to Korea," she continued. "She did not leave until 1945. It was a 'happy interlude' for Korea and Japan."

The history lesson struck Christopher as somewhat mild. After all, it was a fact that these "advances" were actually invasions, acts of military aggression. It was also a fact that thousands of Chinese and Korean civilians had died under Japanese rule. Perhaps, thought Christopher, the teacher wanted to spare the children the brutal truth. That was all right, he figured, as long as they learned the truth at a later time. He thought they probably would.

The teacher now began the lesson on English vocabulary and grammar. The Japanese method of learning languages, Christopher observed, relied almost exclusively on rote memorization and drills. Very little speaking or writing occurred; instead, students memorized words and grammatical rules. Remembering his own boredom when doing grammar exercises, Christopher felt sorry for the students. At that age, he thought, they should be taught language in the form of a game. Conversation and pronunciation could be easy and fun for them, since young children love to imitate. But he realized that this approach would be out of step with the rigid format of Japanese education, and would probably be frowned upon.

The class continued in the same pattern, with students standing to recite. The teacher called on everyone in the room. When a student didn't know the answer or gave a wrong one, the child was corrected and asked to repeat it. Christopher noticed that the children were well behaved, and never spoke out of turn. More surprisingly, they rarely turned to look at him, even though they could tell he was a foreign visitor. Their ability to control their natural curiosity was remarkable, especially considering how young they were.

At the end of the session, the students stood and bowed to the teacher, who bowed in return. First the students silently filed out to join the awaiting *kyoiku-mamas*, and then the teacher left. On the way out, she bowed to Mr. Sakatumi and Christopher.

"The class was very impressive," said Christopher to his host. "Your students are much more advanced than ours at this age. We do not start history lessons until they are seven years old. And we don't require them to learn a foreign language. Our emphasis is on letting them explore the world, within limits of course, and to let their interests guide them. We think an individual's motivation encourages learning."

"In Japan, students must concentrate on lessons in order to pass exams," said Mr. Sakatumi. "In addition to this *juku*, we have a *yobiko*, or 'cramming school,' where students prepare just before the exams. The examination time is very intense— students call it the 'examination hell.' But it is most important to do well, because only those who pass the exam can advance and become successful."

"Let me ask you about teaching methods," said Christopher. "I understand that the American Occupation government tried to reduce the amount of rote learning and replace it with analysis and critical thought. I think the idea was to produce questioning citizens. Didn't that work?"

"Ah, that is American way, not Japanese way," said Mr. Sakatumi. "Each country must be true to itself."

He spoke with a smile and an air of patience, as if everything he said was already quite obvious.

"Well, whatever the Japanese way is, it sure has helped your GNP," said Christopher in an agreeable voice. "I guess you can't argue with success."

As they left the classroom and entered the small courtyard leading to the street, Christopher noticed a small boy looking through the storm fence and staring at the school.

"Is he waiting for someone?" asked Christopher.

"He is *ronin*," replied Mr. Sakatumi. "*Ronin* is a student who has failed examination. He is called *ronin* after the masterless samurai who wandered through forests in ancient Japan. Like *ronin*, such students have no place in society until they pass examination. There is no limit to number of times a student can take examination. System is fair for all. My son is *ronin*."

"What?" exclaimed Christopher. "But your son is in a fine school!"

"Second son fail exam," said Mr. Sakatumi in a matter-of-fact way. "I cannot afford more than one son to attend *juku*. I am very worried that second son will dishonor me. I feel great sorrow."

"That's too bad," said Christopher sympathetically. "But look, maybe he will be successful at a trade or even start up his own business."

"No," said Mr. Sakatumi, again in a neutral tone. "Unless he pass exam, there is no place for him."

Christopher looked back at the young boy behind the fence. He had not moved. It seemed he would be there forever.

Mr. Sakatumi beckoned Christopher to accompany him to the waiting car. As they were driven back to Shinjuku, Christopher reflected on the afternoon's events. The *juku* was impressive in many ways: the children were studious and bright, and the material they were beginning to learn was quite difficult. Christopher admired the dedication and hard work he had seen. Still, his greatest impression was of repetition, regimentation, and memorization. It was clear that the Japanese approach to education was rooted in rote learning. Perhaps, he thought, this was due to the nature of the Japanese language, which demanded a great amount of memorization. In any event, he had not seen any encouragement of personal expression, creativity, or experimentation. The system seemed to prize conformity and discipline, not independence or individuality.

It bothered Christopher that the rigorous examinations began so early and demanded so much. The pressures were severe, particularly when imposed on young children. A student who did poorly at one level—even in the first grade—might never recover. He wouldn't have a chance. Christopher reflected that he himself would have failed in the Japanese system. He had been an average student in high school, but had blossomed into an excellent scholar in college. Yet in Japan, he would have been an outcast, a *ronin* at age fourteen. Christopher's mind drifted home to his small daughter, Sarah. Would he want her to be educated in the Japanese manner? He was not so sure.

The Wanasumi Company car pulled up to Christopher's hotel. Mr. Sakatumi walked him to the entrance, bowed, and said that he would return that evening for dinner. Christopher bowed in return. He noticed how easily he had begun to imitate Japanese custom.

Once back in his room, Christopher lay down on his bed, and thought further about his experiences that day. He had come to respect the Japanese as one of the world's most productive people, yet he was a little uncomfortable with the implications of their approach to education. How was it possible, he wondered, to produce original thinkers or innovators under this system? What would happen to a brilliant nonconformist, to a freethinker who did not yield to the pressures of exams and memorization? He wondered if they, too, would have no place in Japanese society. Perhaps this was why Christopher had never heard of a Japanese inventor like Thomas Edison, or an industrial pioneer like Henry Ford. The Japanese apparently preferred conformity and the perfection of the status quo to independence and the discovery of the future.

He was distracted by the light tap-tap of rain against his hotel window. The skies had darkened and, contrary to the weather report, a storm was about to strike. As the rain came harder, Christopher looked down at the vast city. The neon lights, formerly so crisp in outline, were blurring through the wet windowpane. The city slowly turned into a confusion of colors.

Chapter 5

That evening, Christopher took the elevator down to the lobby. He had a few minutes before Mr. Sakatumi was due to pick him for dinner, and he thought he would relax with a drink in the hotel bar. The itinerary was more tightly organized than he had expected, and the day's activities had left him feeling vaguely tense.

The bar was full of Japanese businessmen, mostly seated at tables, all wearing gray or dark blue suits, some with a hostess keeping them company. Seating himself at the counter, Christopher ordered a drink in halting Japanese. The bartender smiled and replied, "Yes, sir. Extra dry with an olive?"

"Yes, thank you," said Christopher, a little embarrassed.

He paid for the drink and took a sip. As he turned to take a look around the bar he heard a voice say in excellent English, "Are you enjoying your visit to Japan?"

The speaker was a young Japanese man, dressed like the others in a business suit, but sitting off by himself. He smiled warmly but did not bow.

"Oh, yes," said Christopher, somewhat uncertainly. The stranger seemed very friendly, not as formal or distant as Mr. Sakatumi or Mr. Suzuki. Christopher, already somewhat habituated to the protocol of Japanese society, was surprised at his openness.

"My name is Toshiro Yusi," said the young man, extending his hand across the corner of the bar. "But you can call me Ken."

Christopher smiled and returned the handshake. "Well,

pleased to meet you Mr. Yusi—I mean, Ken. Say, how do you come to be called Ken?"

"A friend of mine in the States," he replied, speaking easily and with a very good accent. "I do a lot of traveling in my job, especially to America, and once, on a visit there, Jack decided to give me an American name. Well, it stuck."

"Oh," said Christopher, "that explains why your English sounds so American. What kind of business are you in?"

"I work for a small import–export firm," Ken replied, taking a sip from his drink. "We've got trading partners in America and Europe. What about you?"

"I work with the Covenant Corporation," Christopher answered. "I'm here on a visit, and I'm the guest of the Wanasumi Company."

"I see. And how have you liked Japan so far?"

Christopher was about to answer when he saw Mr. Sakatumi enter the bar. He waved and turned to Ken. "Here comes my host now."

As Mr. Sakatumi joined them, Christopher made the introductions. "Mr. Sakatumi, this is Mr. Ken Yusi. We just met."

Mr. Sakatumi bowed and handed Mr. Yusi a business card. Mr. Yusi pulled two cards from his coat pocket and handed them out. Mr. Sakatumi looked at the card, examining it briefly, then directed a quick question in Japanese to Mr. Yusi. His tone was somewhat curt, as was Mr. Yusi's reply. The exchange continued for several seconds, and became increasingly aggressive in tone. Mr. Sakatumi abruptly returned Mr. Yusi's card and stood angrily, as if to leave.

Mr. Yusi turned to Christopher. "Please forgive this display of rudeness. I hope we'll have the chance to meet again."

He shook Christopher's hand and excused himself. He did not bow to Mr. Sakatumi, but simply walked out of the bar.

Frankly surprised, Christopher turned to Mr. Sakatumi, who bowed toward him and said evenly, "Our car is waiting. Let us go now."

"What was that all about?" asked Christopher as they

walked through the lobby and out to the company car. The chauffeur opened the door and they got in. After an uncomfortable pause, Christopher said, "Was it something I did?"

"It is best not to associate with such a man," replied Mr. Sakatumi, his expression unchanged. "He has brought dishonor upon his family."

"What? He seemed like a nice guy."

"Appearances can deceive," said Mr. Sakatumi.

"Yes, but we were talking about his business trips to America," Christopher continued. "He works for an import-export business—"

"He is like *ronin*. He is *mura hachibu*. He no longer belongs in group because he dishonor family. He has no place."

"What do you mean? What did he do?"

"It is better not to talk about such a man," said Mr. Sakatumi with a tone of finality. Evidently the matter was closed. Christopher wasn't sure what to think—Ken Yusi had seemed so polite and friendly, so Japanese. He hoped that he'd have a chance to talk with Yusi again. For the moment, however, he shifted his thoughts to the upcoming dinner at Mr. Sakatumi's house. He wanted to make a good impression.

"I hope Mrs. Sakatumi didn't go to any extra trouble," said Christopher as the car turned down a street lined with apartment buildings.

"It is no trouble, Mr. Newman," replied Mr. Sakatumi. He spoke to the driver in Japanese and the car slowed to a stop. "We are here," he announced.

They got out of the car and entered the building's small lobby. Christopher had expected that Mr. Sakatumi lived in a free-standing suburban home, like his own, not in a cramped, gray apartment building. The contrast was even more stark when Christopher considered that Mr. Sakatumi was in upper management for a large corporation.

"The scale is certainly different from America," said Christopher as they rode up in the small elevator.

"There is not much space in Japan," replied Mr. Sakatumi.

"Many people live in small apartment. We are fortunate to have a large one."

The elevator doors opened and Christopher followed his host down the tight but immaculately clean hallway. Mr. Sakatumi drew his keys and opened the door at the end of the hall. The smell of cooking met them as they entered what, by American standards, would pass for a small two-bedroom apartment.

Mr. Sakatumi carefully removed his shoes and left them by the door, putting on a pair of slippers. Christopher did likewise, then turned to look around the apartment. The living room consisted of an open area with a low table in the center and a tiny kitchen in an alcove off to one side. The kitchen housed a small washing machine and dryer, a refrigerator, a one-burner gas stove, and an electric rice cooker. A paper partition decorated with calligraphy and simple scenes of nature separated the dining area from the small living room. In the corner sat a little Sony television set and a portable Sanyo cassette tape deck. An air conditioner protruded from beneath the single large window. Just outside was a narrow balcony, accessible through the sliding doors, which the Sakatumis had converted into a miniature garden with bonsai trees, sculptured hedges, and a distinctly Japanese waterfall powered by an electric pump. The waterfall reminded Christopher of the computer-driven chime on the airplane.

"What are those?" asked Christopher, spying two tablets on a shelf over the television.

"Those are ancestral tablets," replied Mr. Sakatumi. "When eldest son marry, he and his wife will live here, to support parents in retirement. When parents die, he will inherit what we have. Ancestral tablets go from father to son."

"But won't your son get his own house?" Christopher inquired.

"Oh, no. Prices too high," answered Mr. Sakatumi. "And son have duty to *uchi*. *Uchi* is like family. Also means company that one works for. Each person has duty to *uchi*."

Christopher realized that the notion of duty, of obligation, was central in Japanese society. The importance of *uchi* was very different from the American emphasis on freedom, on personal independence and self-determination. Just then, Mrs. Sakatumi entered from one of the bedrooms. She bowed to her husband, who turned to Christopher. "This is wife. She has been helping first son with schoolwork. Now she will finish preparing dinner."

Mrs. Sakatumi bowed and turned into the kitchen. Christopher noticed she was carrying a young child on her back. What surprised him was the age of the child—he appeared to be almost two years old. In America, he thought, the youngster would be walking and talking, exploring the world under parental guidance, developing a sense of independence. That was the way he and Nancy were trying to raise Sarah, though it was very difficult at times, and involved both risk and patience. Still, he thought, how else could Sarah develop into an individual?

Christopher watched as Mrs. Sakatumi stirred the tempura vegetables. She put the fish in a strainer, then left the room.

"Please to excuse wife," said Mr. Sakatumi. "She is helping first son with homework. He has another examination next week and must pass. Please, let us sit at table." He knelt at the low table and Christopher joined him, bumping his knees against the table edge.

"What about your other son? Does he have an upcoming exam, too?"

There was an awkward pause.

"Second son is at *yobiko*. He must work to pass entrance exam that he fail."

"Oh. Does Mrs. Sakatumi work?" asked Christopher, eager to change the subject.

"She is *kyoiku-mama*. Her primary duty is to oversee study of children. Sometimes she is worker for Yamashita Electrical Company."

"Sometimes?"

"Yes. Women not have lifetime employment. When no longer needed, women go home. They are temporary workers."

That confirms what I learned at the factory, Christopher thought to himself. It was clear that unlike their American counterparts, Japanese women didn't have much chance to advance in business and rise to the executive level. In fact, Christopher suddenly realized, he hadn't noticed any women at the professional level in Japan. The teacher at the *juku* was a woman, but he wondered how many professors at Tokyo University were female. Probably very few. Women seemed to be relegated to temporary work, or to menial jobs as salesgirls, waitresses, office girls, or elevator attendants—jobs for which they were probably paid half as much as men in comparable positions, and for which there certainly could be no guarantee of employment. Once married, Japanese women seemed to spend their time in the home, like Mrs. Sakatumi, raising the children and becoming education mamas. Christopher knew that some women did make it to the professional ranks, but generally in small companies, and not in larger, established, highly esteemed firms.

Mrs. Sakatumi returned and finished preparing dinner, which she carried over to the table and served without comment. The baby slept on her back.

"Won't your wife be joining us for dinner?" Christopher asked, noticing that there were only two place settings.

"No, she must make sure that son study hard," Mr. Sakatumi answered. Having carefully arranged the food on the table, Mrs. Sakatumi silently left the room, and Christopher and his host served themselves helpings of fish, rice, tempura vegetables, and green tea. Mr. Sakatumi showed his guest how to hold the rice bowl in his left hand, and how to use the chopsticks. Christopher had never been able to use chopsticks easily, and despite the careful instructions, he was awkward at best.

The food was delicious, but conversation was sporadic and

subdued, and the mood was very formal. Mr. Sakatumi said little during the dinner, speaking only when Christopher asked a question, and then only after a silence. Christopher found these silences oppressive, but bore them as best he could, to avoid being rude.

Periodically, Mrs. Sakatumi would emerge silently from the bedroom and bring extra portions from the kitchen to the table, while the baby slept on her back. Once or twice Christopher saw her turn her head and speak softly and musically to the child as he shifted in his sleep, but otherwise the woman said nothing. When her husband spoke to her, it was in a rather formal tone.

Once the meal was over, Mrs. Sakatumi removed the plates and bowls and cleared the table. Mr. Sakatumi poured sake into small porcelain cups and gave one to Christopher, who lifted his cup toward his host and smiled.

"That was a wonderful meal," he said appreciatively.

Mr. Sakatumi bowed his head. "We must drink sake quickly," he said. "It is now 9:15. To meet schedule, car must take you to hotel soon."

"Oh, that's okay," Christopher said. "There's no hurry."

"Yes, but must follow itinerary."

Mr. Sakatumi smiled, drank his sake, and stood up. He bowed to Christopher, who scrambled to his feet and bowed slightly in return. "Please thank your wife for the fine dinner," he said when it became apparent that Mrs. Sakatumi would not be coming out from the bedroom.

Mr. Sakatumi bowed and opened the door. They took the elevator to the ground floor, where Mr. Sakatumi guided his guest to the company car.

"Driver will take you to hotel," he said to Christopher through the window. "Will see you tomorrow at 8 A.M. for next factory tour."

During the drive back to the hotel, Christopher thought about the two-year-old strapped to its mother's back, and of the extended weaning period Japanese children went through.

It was partly because of this, he realized, that the Japanese learned *amae*—dependency on the group. *Amae* would promote conformity and a desire for harmony, and tended to inhibit the desire for independence. And since, as Mr. Sakatumi had said, the company was an extension of *uchi*, or family, *amae* pervaded the workplace, too. No wonder Japanese companies had such loyal workers—they really had been trained, by their culture, to think of large institutions as extensions of the family, and felt a strong sense of dependency and duty. Maybe that was an important reason for their productivity. If everyone did what was necessary to further the ends of the group, then those ends would be achieved. But there could be drawbacks to group dependency, as well.

The car stopped in front of the Keio Plaza Hotel and Christopher walked through the lobby to the elevator. Once in his room, he thought about the differences between Mr. Sakatumi's home life and his own. Not only was the approach to child rearing different, but so was the role of the woman. He wondered how many American women in the 1980s would give up their careers and accept a subservient role. Not very many—he was sure of that. He also thought about the concrete apartment house and cramped living areas. Was that part of the Japanese economic miracle, too?

The phone rang. It was Franklin Ridgeman, calling from Covenant Corporation headquarters.

"Hello, Newman," he said. "How's the mission coming? Have you found it?"

"Well, sir," said Christopher, "I've been doing some research on factories and schools, and—"

"That's fine," said Ridgeman. "As soon as you find the secret, call me collect, okay? I have every confidence you'll find it."

"Uh, thank you, sir," said Christopher, but Ridgeman had already hung up.

Christopher put the phone down and gazed across the hotel room. I've really got a lot of work to do, he thought. It was becoming clear that Japanese culture and values were very different from those in America, and were responsible for shaping Japanese business and management practices. It was just as Mark Truitt had warned him—the interrelation between culture and economics was subtle and complex. If he was going to understand Japanese management techniques, he had to take account of culture, as well.

Christopher was tired, and tomorrow would be another long day. "Wake up at six thirty, breakfast at seven fifteen . . ." He could hear Mr. Sakatumi's voice somewhere in the corridors of his mind. His thoughts began to drift, and soon, still dressed, he fell into a sleep that was neither deep nor restful.

Chapter 6

Christopher awoke the next morning fatigued. He pulled himself out of bed, hurriedly showered and put on fresh clothes, and took the elevator down to the hotel restaurant. Hoping to restore his strength, he ordered eggs, bacon, toast, and coffee. After breakfast he leaned back to collect his thoughts and prepare for Mr. Sakatumi's arrival and the upcoming factory tour.

The previous day had been very valuable, he thought. The Japanese penchant for orderliness and efficiency was everywhere—in the cities, in the factories, in the schools, and even in the home. Some of that efficiency would be useful in America, Christopher reflected. But what struck him most was the marked difference between the two countries. No longer did it seem like an easy task to identify reasons for Japan's economic strength and simply plug them in at the Covenant Corporation. He was sure that there were some management techniques Covenant could borrow from the Japanese, but they had to be carefully selected and judiciously applied. I'll make a special effort to find some today, he said to himself.

"Good morning, Mr. Newman," said a voice behind him. It was Mr. Sakatumi.

"You're right on time," Christopher replied, noticing that it was exactly 8 A.M. He accompanied Mr. Sakatumi out to the car and, after struggling through traffic jams for over an hour, they finally reached their destination—the Nakano Electrical Company, located several miles northeast of Tokyo.

"We have arrived at factory," Mr. Sakatumi announced as the company car neared a tall chain-link fence with barbed wire on top. A pair of guards checked their identification and let them pass through the gate.

"It's immense," said Christopher as he eyed the sprawling complex of buildings extending in every direction. There seemed to be no end to the enormous factory site.

They drove past a series of cement slab buildings, gray and white in color, each with a small row of windows along its upper perimeter, a main entrance at the front, and a small guard station near the door. At the end of the row was Nakano's company headquarters. The car slowed to a stop, and they made their way past the guards toward their waiting host. He was a short, stout man named Mr. Okamura, and he greeted Christopher with a deep bow before exchanging business cards with Mr. Sakatumi.

"I will be here at end of tour," said Mr. Sakatumi. "Please, you may now follow Okamura-san."

Christopher nodded and walked with Mr. Okamura past a set of offices and through a set of double doors onto a factory floor. It was not at all like the manufacturing area at the Toshima Motor Company, Christopher noted. There was no heavy machinery, no huge overhead tracking system, and no overwhelming rhythm of machinery. This factory was simpler, quieter, and bathed in fluorescent light. Here there were far more workers than machines.

"You may have heard of Nakano Electrical Company," Mr. Okamura began in a well-rehearsed voice. "We produce full line of consumer electrical products."

That's putting it mildly, Christopher thought. Nakano was among the best known brand names in the world, and had an outstanding reputation for quality in televisions, component stereos, tape decks, radios, and a variety of other products. It held a large share of the American consumer market, and its growth and success were recognized the world over.

"Over here, Mr. Newman, we have assembly of stereo receivers. Cabinets and front panel are put together here, and components are placed inside finished cabinet at later operation."

"I see," said Christopher. The factory floor was large and crowded, with scores of workers, attired in identical jumpsuits and wearing caps, rushing around the plant.

"Let me ask you something," Christopher continued, deciding to get right to the point. "What do you think are the most important elements of Nakano's success?"

Mr. Okamura smiled. It was a question that many visitors had asked.

"It is due, Mr. Newman, to harmony and cooperation, to policy of lifetime employment, and to Japanese educational system."

Christopher thought for a moment. He already knew that Japanese "lifetime employment" was limited to large firms and didn't extend to women. As such, he knew it wouldn't be acceptable at the Covenant Corporation. And he was familiar with the Japanese schools and their regimentation, intense pressure, and emphasis on rote learning. That wouldn't fit in America, either. But perhaps there were other things that the Covenant Corporation could learn.

Remembering Robert Lagrange's admiration for Japanese production operations, Christopher asked, "Can you please tell me about the management of your production lines?"

"Ah, we use *kanban* system of manufacturing management. It is helpful to reduce costs and ensure quality at all operations."

"What's a *kanban* system?"

"It refers to cards that move with inventory. But it is much more than simple inventory flow system. Nakano factory use 'just-in-time' inventory method. We build parts only as they are needed, and deliver them 'just in time' for next operation. Look."

Mr. Okamura pointed to the nearby work station, where three men were busy putting together a batch of eight cabinets. They quickly finished the lot, then passed it along to the next operation, sending with it a completed *kanban* card. A moment later, a new *kanban* arrived with an order for six more cabinets. The men immediately set about building the new order, and then sent it along, too.

"Fellow employees only build units when they receive *kanban*. Card tells them what model is required and how many to build. Then, when units are complete, they are sent 'just in time' to next operation."

"Does this system ever break down? I mean, what if you don't get the units in time?"

Mr. Okamura smiled. "If a work station does not receive parts that it needs, then there must be failure at previous operation. Problem is quickly identified and then solved. If we had large lot sizes or buffer stock of inventory, we would never discover problem, and would therefore never improve efficiency."

"That's clever," said Christopher. "If you only build what you need for use at the next operation, there can't be any tolerance of error."

"Exactly. Some other companies build extra supplies of parts to make sure that production process can continue. We call this 'just-in-case' inventory. It may seem like good idea, but actually allows for waste. It is better to build only exact quantity and make sure that parts work right."

Christopher watched the line again. An order for a few units arrived, the cabinets were quickly built, and the lot was sent on. The small lot sizes and precise timing helped pinpoint inefficiencies, and helped reduce the cost of carrying inventory.

Just then, a small truck raced through the factory floor and came to a screeching halt a few feet from where Christopher was standing. The driver jumped out and plucked a box from the passenger seat, then handed it to one of the line workers, who ripped the cover off and pulled out a new batch of side panels. He immediately used them to build a new order of receiver cabinets.

Mr. Okamura beamed with satisfaction. "Panels have arrived 'just in time.' If delivery is late, then employees will not be able to complete next order."

"Where did the delivery come from?" asked Christopher.

"From supply company. They provide us with wooden panels, and make delivery at least four times a day. Frequent delivery keep down inventory cost."

"Interesting," said Christopher. The organization and precise coordination between vendor and user was admirable, and clearly increased overall production efficiency. Christopher knew that relations with vendors in America were often unreliable and could stand improvement. Perhaps Lagrange would be interested in adopting this technique at the Covenant Corporation.

Mr. Okamura motioned for Christopher to follow him, and they proceeded down the assembly line. They watched each work station receive a *kanban*, perform the necessary work, and send the small lots on. The reliability of the process was impressive—it reminded Christopher of the TMC plant and its almost machinelike precision. But there was a difference: at TMC the pace of work was dictated by an automated tracking system that moved assemblies to each work station at regular intervals, while at Nakano the relentless pace was determined by *kanban* cards and the demand for "just-in-time" delivery. It was interesting, thought Christopher, that a manufacturing process which responded to order cards could be every bit as fast and pressured as a mechanized one. Like their TMC counterparts, Nakano workers moved at a constant and feverish pace, as new *kanban* cards continually arrived at the work stations.

"Look," said Mr. Okamura, pointing to an operation where one employee was helping another with a complicated task. "That is example of true harmony. One fellow employee help another."

They watched as the assemblers, talking furiously and

working in an urgent fashion, finished the units and sent them to the next operation.

Of course they help each other, Christopher suddenly realized. The workers had to turn out the right number of units in a short amount of time, or else they'd hold up delivery and be identified as a source of trouble. And *nobody* wanted to be responsible for stopping the production line. Teamwork wasn't just a reflection of Japanese spirit and goodwill; it was necessary to keep the production line moving.

As the tour progressed, Christopher thought about the *kanban* inventory management system. This was something that could be of immediate use to the Covenant Corporation. Small lot sizes and timely delivery could cut costs, increase reliability, and minimize scrap and rework expenses. Improved product quality would follow. In addition, a smooth "just-in-time" system would reduce inventory and improve profits. Christopher was pleased with this discovery—it was something the Covenant Corporation would be smart to adopt.

At the same time, Christopher was concerned that Nakano had taken a good idea and carried it too far. Although the *kanban* system improved efficiency, it also imposed excessive pressure on the workers. Employees could no longer vary their pace; each small lot had to be completed in a precise and rapid interval, or the production line would come to a halt. Still, the concept was a good one, and Christopher made careful notes about it.

"Look over here," said Mr. Okamura, interrupting Christopher's thoughts and pointing to a small computer display with graphs and charts appearing on the screen. "Nakano Electrical Company use statistical quality control to achieve reliable process."

"I see," said Christopher. He knew the Japanese were quite sophisticated in their use of statistics. "How long have you been using this approach?"

"Since 1950, Mr. Newman, when Nakano Electrical Company was very small. In that year, Dr. W.E. Deming of United

States visit Japan and teach statistical techniques for manufacturing control. Deming-san very helpful. And in 1954, Dr. J.M. Juran come to Japan to lecture. Juran-san also wise man with many good things to teach Japanese about quality production. Both men are now much honored in Japan."

Mr. Okamura smiled and bowed respectfully as he talked of Deming and Juran, American industrial engineers whose techniques had been more closely followed in Japan than in the United States. How strange, thought Christopher, that Japan learned statistical quality control from America, and was now the world leader in its application. Why hadn't America listened? he wondered.

The tour continued through several more manufacturing areas, and Christopher was struck by the sheer size of the factory and the multitude of workers in it. Nakano employed a staggering number of people.

"Say, Mr. Okamura," Christopher asked, "how do all of these people commute to work? Do they have cars, or do they take buses?"

"Oh, no. They do not have to drive. Company allows them to live here, next to factory. This is not just factory, Mr. Newman—it is a city! Nakano City have housing, schools, and even have stores. We have everything same as city."

"All these people live in houses and apartments on the site?"

"All live on site, Mr. Newman, but not all live in houses or apartments. Single men and women live in dormitories. Would you like to see one?"

"Sure," said Christopher. They left the factory and walked over to a nearby row of four-story barracks.

"These are dormitories," Mr. Okamura announced. "Man will live in this dormitory until married, or until has ten years seniority. This first one is called Lotus Breeze dormitory."

Mr. Okamura escorted Christopher through the building. Each floor had twenty rooms, and each room had twelve bunks. Two hundred and forty men per floor, Christopher calculated in his head, or about a thousand per barrack. He shuddered—it was hard to imagine putting up with this sort of arrangement for ten years. Two years in a college dorm had been enough for him. And it was equally hard to imagine a similar company dorm in the United States. How many Americans would accept this arrangement?

Mr. Okamura pointed out that each room in the Lotus Breeze dormitory had a Nakano company banner, and large *kanji* characters on the walls displayed the company motto: *Order, efficiency, harmony.* "We believe in providing fellow employee with proper environment for productivity," Mr. Okamura said proudly.

They left the dormitory and walked across a service road to a large, low-lying building. As they passed through the doors, Christopher realized they had entered still another factory. This production floor consisted of many long rows of young women, attired in light blue smocks, each sitting at a machine that resembled a large microscope. Each woman peered down through the viewer and used tweezers to move tiny objects around.

"This is semiconductor assembly operation, Mr. Newman. Silicon wafers are fabricated in nearby plant, and chips are brought here for attachment to lead frame. These girls bond chip to frame before plastic molding."

The young women sat squeezed together, with hardly enough room to move. Christopher noticed that the factory was strangely silent, with no one talking and no sound of equipment, but the pace of work was frantic nonetheless. The women worked quickly, never pausing, and were seemingly absorbed in their jobs. There were at least 800 women on the production floor, each repeating the same operation over and over.

Other women pulling small carts proceeded briskly up and down the aisles, stopping at particular spots and delivering or collecting batches of chips. First they brought racks of chips and new lead frames with *kanbans* attached, and minutes later they returned to collect the assembled work. It was the same system Christopher had seen throughout the Nakano Electrical Company, but was even more cramped and crowded.

"High volume and fast assembly mean low unit cost," said Mr. Okamura, gesturing to the vast rows of workers with a wave of his arm. "We call this economy of scale."

"No wonder Japan is becoming so strong in semiconductors," Christopher said. "This sort of operation must really keep your costs down." He glanced around at the hundreds of laborers on the production floor. The factory was cramped and the atmosphere was stifling.

"Ah, but Japan not so strong anymore," said Mr. Okamura. "We face grave threat."

"Oh? How's that?" Christopher said in a surprised voice.

"We face grave threat from Korea, Mr. Newman. Koreans have even larger plants, with more operators, and pay less to workers. They are very organized and disciplined people. We fear that they will become less expensive producer than Japan, and will overtake us."

"What? Are you sure?" asked Christopher.

"Yes, afraid so. Already Korea is more efficient than Japan at production of steel. Also strong in shipbuilding, and now beginning to export automobiles. Other industries will follow. I fear that Japan will have to become more efficient, make production line even faster, use greater economy of scale, to keep up with Korea."

Christopher stopped short, taken aback. For the last several years, American industry had held up the Japanese as a model of success, and was trying to learn from their example. In some areas, Christopher had discovered, the Japanese model could be instructive, but in other instances it involved vast cultural differences, or relied on extreme working conditions, relentless pressure, and low pay.

Now, it appeared, even becoming like the Japanese wouldn't be enough, since the Koreans could produce at a still lower cost. Where would it all end? At some point the human and social costs would outweigh any financial gains. There must be another way, Christopher thought. Trying to become just like the Japanese, or like the Koreans, couldn't be the only alternative.

Mr. Okamura walked Christopher back to the front office and turned him over to Mr. Sakatumi. The ride back to Shinjuku was slow and uneventful. Traffic was heavy, and Christopher could see commuter buses and rapid transit trains packed full of workers, going home after a long day's work.

Even the traffic moved with a purpose and intensity. It was as though all of Tokyo was an immense *kanban* system, with vehicles and people moving like so many pieces of inventory, striving to reach their destinations "just-in-time." The frenzied street traffic and the pressured factory were both reflections of the Japanese obsession with organization and efficiency.

Christopher sighed and looked out the window. The day's experiences had only increased his fatigue, and tomorrow there was yet another tour of another factory. He sensed his weariness and looked forward to getting a good night's sleep.

Chapter 7

Entering the lobby, Christopher heard music and loud conversation coming from the hotel lounge. Maybe a drink will help me relax before I go to my room, he thought. He walked up to the bar and ordered a drink.

"Hello, again," said a voice behind him. It was Ken Yusi.

"Hi," said Christopher. "Nice to see you again. Care to join me?"

"Okay," Yusi replied, "but the drinks are on me." He ordered a drink for himself and paid the bartender. "After all," he said, smiling, "you're our guest here."

"Thanks," said Christopher appreciatively, "but the next round's on me."

Ken took a sip from his drink.

"Say," he asked, "how's the visit going? Have you learned much about Japanese management? Anything you can take back to the States?"

"Well," Christopher replied, "I don't know." He stared into his drink. "I'm just not sure what to think anymore. I've seen some impressive things here, but I just don't know how much of the Japanese system we can use in America. There seem to be such basic differences between our countries."

Yusi paused for a moment. He looked at Christopher thoughtfully.

"You know, Chris, you're the first American I've heard say that. Most Americans are sold on Japan before they really understand it. They're sure that America can restore its economic health by imitating the Japanese."

"Well, uh, what do you think?" Christopher asked hesitantly.

"Oh, I agree with you," Yusi replied quickly. "I've traveled to America and I know the differences are deep. But not many Americans see this—or want to. Let me give you an example. In my former job I worked for a steel company that made the rails for our 'bullet train.' A group of Americans who wanted to build a similar rail system between Los Angeles and San Diego came to see how our train worked, and I was asked to be host to them on part of their tour. Well, the train is impressive—it's fast, efficient, and reliable. The Americans admired the control center, and they absolutely loved the train. They were ready to go back to California and begin building one right away."

"What's wrong with that?" asked Christopher. "It sounds like something you should be proud of."

"We are proud of it. But there are problems with the system that don't appear at first glance."

"What sort of problems?" Christopher asked.

"Well," Yusi responded, "the train passes through the city, right next to apartments and houses. Families living there couldn't get any sleep, windows rattled, and as the foundations of many houses gradually shifted under the vibrations the flooring buckled. The transit authority reinforced the buildings, built walls to block out the sound, and installed vibration barriers, but it hasn't helped."

"Didn't the Americans notice the train's route and ask about its effect on the neighborhoods?" Christopher asked.

"No, they didn't," said Yusi.

"That's strange," Christopher replied, taking a swallow from his drink. "You would think that Americans would be sensitive to environmental problems."

"The Americans were blind," Yusi said, "because they wanted to be. They seemed so sure that the Japanese bullet trains were the answer that they just looked the other way. What's more, the Americans didn't seem interested when I mentioned that the system was starting to run in the red because of rising labor costs. I thought they'd be very concerned about that, given higher labor costs in America. But they weren't."

"You know, people are sometimes blind," said Christopher. "I'm trying to be objective, but it's hard, especially when the weight of American business opinion is on the other side. I'm beginning to feel that Americans think that *anything* the Japanese do is right, because, after all, no one can argue with your rapid economic growth."

"Yes, our economic growth has been rapid," said Yusi, "but there have also been inevitable, not so desirable by-products of economic growth. In Yokkaichi there was so much smog one year it induced mass asthma. And of course you know about the mercury poisoning at the fishing village of Minimata. But there are other things, too. We Japanese love nature, yet we often deface mountains by building 'skyline drives' for tourists. We have what we call 'renowned beauty spots,' but we bury them beneath hotels and trinket shops. Things got so bad that we recently developed the concept of *kogai*. It's a political concept of 'public injury' that attempts to solve some of these problems. But there hasn't been much progress so far."

Yusi turned and called for the bartender.

"Hey, these are on me," Christopher said with a smile, giving the bartender the order. They waited for the drinks, then resumed their conversation.

"You know," Yusi said, "Americans always point out that Japan's GNP is very high. But most Japanese think that GNP is really a misleading statistic. Our GNP looks good unless you take into consideration the pollution, the overcrowding, and Japan's total dependence on raw materials from other countries. The standard of living, measured statistically, looks impressive. But the average quality of life is low when compared with America or Europe. I doubt if many Americans would want to actually live like the Japanese."

"Well, I did notice how small Mr. Sakatumi's apartment

was," Christopher commented. "I didn't actually see the bedrooms, but they had to be small, too, judging from the studio-sized front room and kitchen."

"What you saw was a relatively big apartment," Yusi replied. "Land prices here are extremely high, and a typical Japanese family apartment is no bigger than an American studio apartment. And only half the people in Tokyo have access to flush toilets. Many things Americans take for granted just don't exist in Japan."

"I'm beginning to see some of the realities myself," Christopher said. "I saw a production line at the Toshima Motor Company where the workers were really pressured. On the surface there seemed to be great teamwork and harmony, but it wasn't hard to see the tension below. I got the definite impression that if you fouled up the assembly line you would be persona non grata."

"That's true," said Yusi. "There are lots of hidden problems Americans don't see, and they're not limited to the production line. They occur at the managerial level, too. For example, Japanese managers are promoted very slowly: a dozen new employees hired together from the university can work for ten years before any of them get promoted. Some Americans have said that slow promotions are good, since development takes time. But it also means that employees get no reward for ten years, regardless of how they perform."

"I don't think many Americans would appreciate that," Christopher noted. "After all, the American system is based on reward for individual achievement."

Ken smiled. "Many Japanese dislike it, too. It can breed great resentment and tension. But no one dares show it, because disturbing the appearance of harmony is dishonorable. That's why I got out of the game."

"What?" Christopher asked. "What do you mean, 'got out of the game'?"

"I quit my job at Taki Steel Company, one of Japan's leading firms. It was an almost unheard-of thing to do. No one quits a job with a good company in Japan—to quit is to dishonor your family."

"Are you serious?" Christopher said in disbelief.

"Sure. Why do you think your host became so angry last night? He saw on my card that I work for a small firm, and asked if I had been to the university. I told him that I was a graduate of Tokyo University, and then joined Taki Steel. He asked why I was no longer with them, and I told him I had quit. Then he became furious and refused my card."

"He was upset, all right," said Christopher. "He told me not to associate with you. He called you a *mura hachibu.*"

"It's too bad, but that's a common reaction," said Ken philosophically.

"And all because you left your job?" Christopher asked. "That's crazy."

He was beginning to get irritated with Japanese business practices. The more he looked at them, the more petty and tyrannical they seemed.

"To some parts of Japanese society, I'm an outcast," Ken continued. "It all stems from our emphasis on hierarchy. Have you ever wondered why Japanese are constantly exchanging business cards? It's to show position and establish rank. The cards are designed to clarify a man's position and group affiliation—like 'Managing Director of Fuji Bank' or 'Professor of Economics, Tokyo University.' Hierarchy, and knowing your place in it, is very important in Japan. That's why, even if your supervisor is wrong or incompetent, you do what he says. You can silently disagree, but you cannot disobey."

"So when you quit, you were in effect rejecting the whole hierarchy, the culture itself," said Christopher.

"In effect, yes. But I'm happy I did it. The emphasis on conformity just got to me. So I went to work for a small import-export company. We do most of our business with America so I'm abroad a lot. In my own country, I'm what you'd call a pariah, but I'm doing what I want to do. And who knows, I may even go a step further and try to start up my own import-export company. The idea appeals to me."

"I can't get over it," Christopher said. "You're considered a pariah for doing what Americans do all the time."

Christopher stirred his drink and looked around. The room was crowded now, and the after-work party was at its height. The patrons seemed like any other group of people trying to relax. He looked back at his friend. Ken's attitude seemed so different, so exceptional for a Japanese. Perhaps he had been shaped by a unique experience.

"You sound awfully critical of your country," Christopher remarked, a bit puzzled.

Ken put his glass down and laughed. "I suppose it sounds that way," he said, shaking his head, "but, really, I love Japan very much. I'm very fond of traditional Japanese art and the-ater, and I travel a lot through the islands, learning about our history and people. In many ways, I'm really more of a tradi-tionalist than a radical. And there are many positive aspects to Japanese life, including the very low level of crime. So don't misunderstand me—this is my home, and this is where I'm happiest. But I don't accept the rigidity and pressure of mod-ern Japanese society, and I don't like what the emphasis on economic success is doing to our country. And I'm not alone in this opinion. Many of our artists, like Mitsuo Yanagimachi, the filmmaker, focus their work on the erosion of our tradi-tional cultural and spiritual values. Even the new program of 'Living National Treasures' which supports practitioners of the traditional arts—like calligraphers and potters—is a sign that the subordination of man to machine has gone too far in Japan."

Christopher nodded. Clearly Japan was a land of paradox—much more complex than it first appeared to a foreigner. And he didn't envy Ken's position as an outsider in his own country.

Christopher finished his drink and looked around the bar again.

"No women in this bar," he remarked, "except for the hostesses."

"It's common in Japan for people who work together to go out for a drink after work," said Yusi. "That's when a lot of decision making occurs. But women aren't invited. It's part of the sexism that pervades Japanese society. Opportunities for women are rare, and if a woman manages to rise in the hierarchy, she is under intense pressure. But most women never get that far. My sister, for example, is more talented than I am, but has remained an office flower, a *shokuba no hana*. Her job is to serve as an ornament."

"But why should that happen?" Christopher asked. "If she's capable, why won't her managers promote her?"

"Because they cannot let a woman supervise men," replied Yusi. "A woman must stay in her place. If she rejects this, she can be ostracized."

"Like you? She could be a pariah?" Christopher asked.

"Yes, and it can be unpleasant," Yusi said. He smiled. "Pressures are even greater, though, for the factory workers—people who can't just quit or easily get another job."

"Well, I've seen some of the pressure production workers are under. Is that what you mean?"

"It's more than that," Ken replied. "For one thing, employees are subjected to heavy doses of indoctrination. You know—company songs, organized exercises, and company slogans. There are even weekend retreats to immerse the employees in company values. And some corporations provide cheap housing to keep the workers right next to the factory."

"That's right," Christopher said. "I saw company dorms at Nakano City. They didn't seem like very pleasant places to live."

Ken nodded in agreement. "The company also provides vacation spots for use by groups of employees. Even sports teams and organized races are encouraged, to make the lives of workers center as much as possible on the company. You see, if the employee is made to identify with the company, then he won't identify with his skill, and that in turn undermines the development of Western-style unions. Unions in Japan are company unions—they almost always do what management wants."

"No strikes, I'll bet," Christopher said, remembering the docile company union at TMC.

"None at all," replied Yusi. "The only real strikes, in the American sense, occurred in the fifties. There have been none since then."

"But are the workers happy with that?" Christopher asked. "After all, the interests of management and labor aren't always the same."

"On the surface, Japanese workers always seem happy," said Yusi. "They are 'happy' to work overtime, they don't use up vacation time, and it looks like they're always faithful to the company. Actually, they have little choice. In many company dormitories there are supervisors who keep constant watch on the activities of the employees, even in their rooms. The company takes an active interest in anything that might affect the employee's productivity. Supervisors enter rooms without warning and employees are pressured to inform on each other. And if you quit, you lose all your seniority and start at an entry-level job at another company. There's good reason why Japanese employees seem so loyal—they really have no choice, practically speaking."

Christopher placed his glass on the counter. He felt relaxed around Yusi, and his energy had returned. There was something reassuring about Ken's philosophical calm; it reminded him of Mark Truitt. And Yusi seemed to have a realistic grasp of Japanese business that Christopher could respect. He understood both the good and the bad.

"I really appreciate your help," Christopher said. "I'm starting to see Japan from another angle."

"Appearance and reality are not necessarily the same thing," Yusi observed. "What you may have read or seen about Japan in the media is oversimplified. Our economic success has given us a positive image in America, but in the rest of the world, particularly Asia, our success has made us enemies."

"You mean the Chinese?" asked Christopher. He knew the Chinese and the Japanese had a traditional enmity.

"No, actually we get along with China fairly well," said Yusi. "It's other countries who see us achieving economically what we lost militarily. The Koreans and Filipinos, for instance, still remember us as colonial masters and wartime conquerors. They still have a lot of bitterness toward the Japanese—a recent goodwill tour to the Philippines by the Prime Minster resulted in anti-Japanese riots."

"American opinion about Japan has its detractors too," Christopher said, thinking about his conversation with Hornblower. "Many Americans resent the Japanese for not paying their share of their own defense, and for the favorable trade balance they enjoy with the United States. That's why many Americans want protectionist laws against Japanese imports."

"Yes, it was inevitable," Yusi said. "Limiting imports is another example of *wa*, or the need for group harmony, that dominates Japanese society. In business, this means that foreign imports are minimized and Japanese firms are given preferential treatment. Japanese firms compete vigorously against each other, but because of *wa*, will band together in the face of foreign competition. The bottom line is, the preservation of Japan must come first." There was a tone of resignation in his voice.

"Say," Ken said after a while, "I've got some free time tomorrow. What does your day look like?"

"Well," said Christopher, "according to my itinerary, Mr. Sakatumi is going to take me on a tour of a zipper factory at 8 A.M. But, you know, I'd just as soon skip it. I think I've seen enough factories for the time being."

"That's great," said Yusi. "Do you like sports?"

"Sure," replied Chris.

"O.K., tell you what," Yusi said. "There's a sumo match tomorrow evening that starts at eight o'clock. Would you like to go? Sumo is a traditional Japanese sport—my favorite, in fact."

"Sounds good," Christopher said.

"And if you like we can start by going to see a baseball game in the afternoon. I think you might like to see how baseball is played in Japan."

"An American import, eh?" Christopher joked. "I'd love to go to a game."

"I'll be by to pick you up tomorrow morning, then," said Ken, rising from his seat. They shook hands and walked from the bar, Ken leaving the hotel and Christopher making his way to his room. He was feeling a lot better, and was particularly happy to find Yusi warm and friendly, not distant and formal, like Mr. Sakatumi.

Once in his room, Christopher called Mr. Sakatumi's house and got a phone answering machine. He didn't understand a word of Japanese, but knew that he should leave his message at the sound of the beep. A delicate Japanese chime sounded, and he left word informing Mr. Sakatumi that he would not be available the next day, and that he would soon be in touch. He hung up the phone. For a change, he felt relaxed and comfortable.

Later that night Christopher was jolted awake from a sound sleep by the insistent ringing of the telephone. Still half asleep, he fumbled for the set.

"Hello?" he said groggily.

"Newman! Is that you?"

"What? Hello?"

"This is Lagrange! Have you found it yet?"

"What?" He was now sitting upright in his bed, trying to clear his head.

"The secret! You know, Newman, the secret of Japanese productivity! Have you found it yet?"

"Oh. Uh, what time is it?"

"Time? What time is it? Why, it's twelve noon! What's the matter with you? Have you been sleeping?"

"Uh, no, sir. I, uh . . ."

"Are you lying down on the job, Newman? The Covenant Corporation is depending on you and so is Bob Lagrange. Now get out there and find that secret!"

Before Christopher could answer, Lagrange hung up. Christopher put the phone back on the hook and glanced at the clock. It was 3 A.M., Tokyo time. He sat for a moment, then leaned back into his pillow. He didn't feel like sleeping.

Chapter 8

Christopher was waiting at the curb the next day when Ken's small car pulled up. The two men exchanged greetings, and Christopher got in for the drive to the baseball stadium. It was a pleasant day, warm and sunny, and there was only a moderate amount of smog in the air.

"The game begins at one," said Ken as he pulled out into the busy streets of Shinjuku, "but I thought it would be interesting to get out to the park a few hours early. I have a friend who's a sportswriter for a local paper, and he agreed to show us around before the game."

"That sounds fine," Christopher answered. "I'm looking forward to a long afternoon out at the ballpark. I think some relaxation would be good for me—I've been spending most of my time on factory tours!"

They drove to Korakuen Stadium in north-central Tokyo and made their way to the press box on the second deck. Ken quickly found his friend, sitting and reading the box scores from the previous day's game.

"Chris, this is Yoshi Kanatsu. We're old friends from high school days."

Yoshi smiled warmly. "Nice to meet you, Chris," he said in very good English. "Have you been to a baseball game in Japan before?"

"No, this is my first time," said Christopher. "But I've seen lots of games in America."

"Well, the rules are the same, but we play the game a little differently over here. Come on, let's take a look around the park."

Yoshi rose from his chair and guided Christopher and Ken to an elevator that carried them down to the clubhouse level. They walked along a tunnel and emerged through the first-base dugout onto the playing field. Christopher paused and looked around at the stadium. There was nothing unusual about it—a double-decked baseball stadium with about 40,000 seats, and a large scoreboard towering above the outfield. Except for the many large advertisements that stood out in bold Japanese characters, Korakuen Stadium could have passed for an American park.

The field was swarming with players and coaches of both teams. Ballplayers were busily practicing hitting and fielding, doing calisthenics, and exercising at full speed, all under the close supervision of their coaches. It was a scene of intense activity and motion.

"I've never seen both teams practicing on the field at once," Christopher remarked. "In the United States, the teams take turns before the game."

"That isn't possible here," Yoshi answered, "since there isn't enough time to take turns. Each team practices for four hours before every game."

"Four hours? Are you kidding?"

"It's true. Japanese teams emphasize superior conditioning and practice all aspects of the game constantly. The players are just as competitive and hard-working during practice as they are during the games, since they want their coaches to know they are serious and capable of producing."

Christopher watched the intensity of the pre-game drill. It was a far cry from the often relaxed and informal warmups he had seen in the United States. Nobody chewed tobacco or talked casually with other players or reporters. Everyone concentrated on his particular activity, and often furiously so—pitchers scarcely paused between pitches, and hitters swung as often as possible, bringing the bat back to an upright position with exaggerated quickness.

"Not all people agree on the benefits of four-hour drills,"

Yoshi continued. "Many players tell me that they are already very tired when it is time for the game to begin. And we often see players become exhausted by mid-season. There are some suggestions that the pre-game exercises be shortened, so that players won't get so worn out. But the team management believes that repetition is the key to perfection, and the players do not wish to disagree with their coaches, since preserving harmony is most important. No player would dare disagree with his coach."

Christopher smiled and shook his head. "The Japanese approach to sports sounds an awful lot like their style of business management," he said to Yusi. "The repetition, the pressure, preserving the appearance of harmony—I've seen all of that in factories. But I didn't think it extended to sports, too."

"It shouldn't be too surprising if you think about it," Ken observed.

Christopher nodded without speaking.

The three men strolled among the ballplayers, and walked down the right field line toward the bull pen. They passed players doing stretching exercises, doing sit-ups and push-ups, and running wind sprints. All exercised at full steam, and most were covered with sweat. Coaches watched their every move, sometimes glancing down at stopwatches to monitor the players' actions. Christopher looked up at the large Seiko clock above the center field stands and noticed that there were still two hours before game time. The workout was only half over.

Yoshi pointed to a tall left-handed pitcher throwing in the bull pen. "That is Kenji Nokobe. He will be the starting pitcher today."

"Why is he warming up now if he's the starting pitcher?" Christopher asked. "He'll wear out his arm if he keeps throwing this hard before the game."

"Oh, it is customary for pitchers to throw every day. Nokobe will throw 500 pitches on most days. Today, since he is the starter, he will throw only 300 times in practice. He will pitch at full speed for two hours."

"But that's crazy!" Christopher exclaimed. "He'll ruin his arm at that rate. American pitchers throw fewer than 150 pitches during a game, and don't throw much between outings. They'd hurt their arms if they worked out like this!"

"Yes, I agree with you," said Yoshi. "But the coaches believe otherwise. Nokobe has a good fastball, and the pitching coach believes that if he throws it often enough, he will perfect it."

"Not everything improves with practice," said Christopher in a low voice, shaking his head in amazement. He paused and looked back at Nokobe, who kept on firing his fastball at top speed. Two coaches kept him under close watch.

On the way back to the dugout, Yoshi mentioned that several American major leaguers had come to play professional baseball in Japan. A few, he said, were excellent players and big favorites with the fans. "Japanese fans are very fond of powerful hitters and admire their long home runs," he added.

"Are there any Americans playing on these teams?" Christopher asked.

"Yes, the Carps have an American on their team—Lefty Hawkins, the pitcher."

Christopher was surprised. "Hawkins? Do you mean it? Lefty Hawkins was a very good pitcher when he played for Chicago. How is he adjusting to playing baseball over here?"

"There are problems, I'm afraid," Yoshi said. "Look, there's Lefty now."

Yoshi pointed toward the dugout, where a tall American player stood next to a Japanese coach. Hawkins was waving his arms; occasionally he pointed to the mound. He appeared to be protesting something. Suddenly his voice got louder.

"Are you kidding? I've got a pulled hamstring muscle and there's no way I can practice! I've got to get some rest if I'm going to pitch tomorrow!"

"All players must practice same way," said the coach, speaking with a heavy accent. "Is bad for harmony on team to make exception."

"But that's not the point," countered Hawkins. "The point

is this: do you want me to win tomorrow or not? I know the best way to prepare myself for a game."

"That is not so," the coach replied evenly. "Coach know best. You must do as you are told. You are not American ballplayer anymore. You are Japanese player."

"Oh, give me a break!" Hawkins cried in exasperation. He turned and stormed off.

Christopher quickly walked over and introduced himself.

"Man, am I glad to see you!" said the American ballplayer with a look of relief. "It's nice to see a friendly face. You can't believe the rules they have over here! It's oppressive! I'm surprised I can put up with it at all."

"Has it been hard to adjust to the Japanese way?" asked Christopher.

"You wouldn't believe what it's like!" said Lefty. "We start each day with a team meeting where each player has to 'dedicate himself' to do a better job in the next game. And anyone who made a key error in the previous game is pointed out and shamed. Can you believe that? And then we come out to the park for these incredible workouts. They're unbelievable! I mean, practice is great, but enough is enough! We're drenched with sweat and damn near dead by game time. And then we have team meetings in the dugout three times a game, to discuss our performance. Why can't they just let us play ball?"

Christopher shrugged sympathetically.

"And that's not all!" Hawkins continued. "We're supposed to be a 'harmonious unit' so they make us do just about everything together. We eat together, travel together, and we even sleep together in one big room. And no one can ever get upset about anything, because we're supposed to be examples of harmony and good behavior."

"Well," said Christopher, "what about the quality of play in Japan? Are the Japanese ballplayers as good as Americans?"

"No, they aren't," Hawkins replied, taking off his cap and scratching his head in bewilderment. "That's what I don't understand. They go through all this effort to be disciplined, and they still don't play very well. It's funny. The New York Yankees, with all of their bickering, were a terrific team a few years back. So were the Oakland A's in the early seventies, when they used to have arguments and fights and everything. Sometimes a team does best if it just lets the players do their own thing."

Just then, a Japanese coach walked up and barked an order at Lefty, who rolled his eyes and shook his head. "Well, gotta go now. If I don't run a few laps they'll say I've dishonored the team!"

With that, Lefty Hawkins trotted off and began jogging around the perimeter of the field. At one point he waved to a few fans. Christopher walked back to where Ken and Yoshi were standing and accompanied them back up to the press box, where they watched the completion of the drill and ate a box lunch of fish and rice. Not quite the same thing as hot dogs and peanuts, thought Christopher, but good nevertheless.

The stands slowly filled as game time approached. At last, the Tokyo Carps took the field and the umpire shouted "Pooray Boru." The Kobe Whalers sent their batters to the plate and threatened to score in the very first inning—they had a man at second base with two outs, and their powerful first baseman was up next.

"This is an extremely critical situation," said Yoshi in a hushed voice. A stillness fell over the ballpark; fans and writers alike leaned forward with excitement.

"Why is it so critical?" asked Christopher. "This is only the first inning. Even if the Whalers score, the Carps have plenty of time to catch up."

"That is true," replied Yoshi, "but in Japan, much importance is placed on scoring the first run of the game. The team that scores first is thought to have gained a psychological advantage, and the other team is said to have lost face."

The batter worked the count to two balls and two strikes, then hit an easy groundball toward the shortstop. It should have been fielded for the final out of the inning, but the short-stop booted the ball, allowing the runner to score from second base. The crowd gasped; the visitors had scored first. Right away, a player dashed out of the Carp's dugout and ran toward the infield, and the man who had missed the grounder rushed off the field.

"The manager is replacing the player who cost us the first run," explained Yoshi. "This is a common move: a player who makes a mistake or fails to perform at an important time is often removed from the game at once. The manager must attempt to compensate for the loss of face."

Making an error on the field was sort of like shutting down the production line, thought Christopher. There was peer pressure and humiliation in either case. One mistake and you were gone.

The Carps tied the score at 1–1 in the first inning, but the Whalers scored four runs in the second, and added five more in the third to take a commanding lead. Kenji Nokobe, the Carps's pitcher who had looked so strong in practice, was tiring on the mound, and the Whalers had no problem hitting his pitches. He was tired and worn down when finally relieved in the fourth inning.

Americans like to think of baseball as part of their tradition, Christopher mused, a reflection of their national character. But here in Japan, the game seemed to reflect Japanese values. And from what Lefty Hawkins had said, the penchant for discipline and order wasn't producing a better brand of baseball.

The Whalers went on to win the game by a score of 12 to 5. The crowd quietly left the stadium. Christopher and Ken thanked Yoshi for his hospitality, then walked out to their car.

"Did you enjoy the game?" asked Ken.

"Very much," Christopher said, "although it wasn't exactly what I expected. And I'd hate to be the fellow who missed the groundball in the first inning!"

Ken nodded as he pulled out of the parking lot and began weaving his way through the busy traffic.

"Do we have a long way to go before we reach the sumo stadium?" Christopher asked.

"Oh, yes. We're going clear across Tokyo," Ken told him. "We're going to the Kuramae Kokugan Hall, next to the Sumida River on the eastern side of the city. It's the most famous sumo hall in Tokyo. There's even a sumo museum right next to it."

"Sort of like a Hall of Fame?" Christopher wondered.

"Yes, like that. Sumo has a very rich heritage. It has a long history and important place in Japanese culture."

"Well, I hope it's not too hard to follow."

"Oh, no," Ken assured him. "It's very simple. There are very few rules that you have to know. I'll explain them to you when we get there."

"By the way," Ken added, "we're going to an important tournament today. There will be several matches between our finest wrestlers, called *sekitori*. One match, in particular, is very important—the present champion, Nakahara, will face the former champion, Amaratsu. Everybody's been looking forward to this rematch.

"There is also a personal angle involved. The defending champion is a young man, only twenty-five years old. When he was just beginning, he studied under Amaratsu. So you see, it is the teacher who is now trying to recover the championship from his former student."

"Is there any animosity between them?" Christopher inquired.

"Oh, no. They are neither enemies nor friends. Personality does not enter into this competition."

Ken pulled up to a red light and they watched the cross traffic pass by. Taxis, trucks, and private cars all sped by with the intensity and purpose that Christopher had come to know. The traffic never seemed to let up.

After the light turned, Ken accelerated and continued talking about the upcoming bout.

"In his early days, Nakahara had a reputation as a talented but unsuccessful warrior. He improved greatly while studying under Amaratsu. Then, after leaving Amaratsu, he proceeded to train with a circle of advisers, and developed a dedicated and rigorous approach to the sport. Now he has become our finest *sekitori*, thanks to his single-minded and disciplined attitude."

"What kind of a wrestler is Amaratsu?" Christopher asked.

"Oh, he is good, too," Ken answered. "His style is not as disciplined as Nakahara's, but he is clever and wily. So this will be a match of contrasting styles, too."

Ken looked out to his left and motioned with his hand. "Over there, Chris, you can see Tokyo University. And nearby is Ueno Park. It is a very pretty and very traditional Japanese park."

"Well, maybe I'll have a chance to see it before I leave Tokyo," said Christopher.

They reached the Kuramae Kokugan Arena and Ken parked the car. They passed through the gates and soon found their box seats in the section marked *masuseki*. It was a simple arena, Christopher noted, not as large as he had expected, and it was already filled with spectators. At the center of the arena was a small circular ring, no more than fifteen feet in diameter.

Ken motioned toward the ring. "That is the *dohyo*. It's made of bales of straw covered with dirt, and provides a good surface for wrestling. The rules of sumo are very simple: a match is won when a contestant is either forced out of the *dohyo*, or touches the ground with any part of his body other than his feet."

"That's a lot simpler than our wrestling," Christopher noted.

"Yes, it is very easy to understand," said Ken with a smile. "Ah, here are *sekitori* entering ring."

Christopher watched as the wrestlers, a dozen in all, strode to the ring and stood in a circle around the perimeter. Each was wearing a beautifully embroidered silk apron over his loincloth. Ken explained that the ceremony, called the *dohyo-iri*, demonstrated the wrestlers' intent to fight fairly and to drive evil spirits out of the ring. The ceremony soon ended and the warriors cleared the ring.

"Ah!" said Ken, nudging Christopher and pointing toward the *dohyo*. "Here's the *gyoji*, the judge. He acts as referee during the bouts. Five other judges will sit at ringside to decide any disputes."

The judge, dressed in a ceremonial silk robe, entered the ring and tossed a handful of salt on the ground. Ken explained that this was intended to purify the *dohyo* and was an important part of sumo tradition. Two large *sekitori* then entered the ring for the first match of the day, and took positions on opposite sides of the *dohyo*. They were both massive, tall by Japanese standards, each weighing over 300 pounds. They wore only loincloths, and their black hair was tightly drawn into a topknot.

The wrestlers crouched and faced each other. At the judge's signal, they drove forward with terrific force and locked in a powerful embrace. The two men pushed, grabbed, pulled, and groaned, striving to get a positional advantage, straining to gain leverage. After several seconds, one warrior managed to push the other over and force his arm to touch the ground. The judge pointed his fan to signal that the match was over, and the crowd applauded appreciatively.

Several more matches followed. Christopher sat absorbed, marveling at the power and agility of the *sekitori*, while his friend explained some subtleties of the sport and offered stories and background about several combatants. Ken seemed to know a lot about sumo and clearly enjoyed its lore and traditions. How ironic, Christopher thought, that someone who loved this most Japanese of sports would be considered an outcast by traditional Japanese society simply for changing jobs.

Finally it was time for the match between Nakahara and Amaratsu. The *gyoji* again sprinkled the ring with salt, and the two famous wrestlers strode into the ring. Christopher could sense the anticipation and excitement in the arena; and the crowd grew silent and tense.

"That's the reigning champion, Nakahara, on the left," Ken whispered. "And Amaratsu is the smaller man on the right. It will be a best two-out-of-three match to determine the championship."

"Who do you think will win?" asked Christopher in a hushed tone.

"It's hard to say," Ken replied evenly. "Let's watch."

The crowd was still and all eyes were on the two warriors, who finished their preparations and took their positions at opposite sides of the *dohyo*. Nakahara was a huge man, with great rounded shoulders and an enormous protruding belly. The gentle curves of his torso belied its enormous power. His expression was determined and severe; as Ken had said, the champion seemed a disciplined and single-minded fighter. Amaratsu, by contrast, was smaller, and moved nervously as he anticipated the opening signal.

The first match began as the two men locked in a clinch, arms extended, legs planted apart, centers of gravity low, grappling and driving with full force. After several seconds, Nakahara's greater size and strength became too much for the older man, and he drove Amaratsu back across the ring, finally pushing him clear out of the *dohyo* with a mighty shove. Slowly, shaken but not hurt, Amaratsu came to his feet and walked around in bewildered circles, while Nakahara bowed mechanically to the crowd. He had dominated the first round.

"Nakahara is in good form today," said Ken, nodding seriously. "He has trained hard."

"He looks unbeatable," Christopher agreed. It was hard to imagine Nakahara losing to anyone—he was too strong and solid, and looked as immovable as the Great Pyramid.

The second match also began with a clinch, but this time

Amaratsu refused to match strength with the larger man. Instead, he relied on his quickness, his agility, and his balance. He moved continuously, shifting directions, reacting swiftly to Nakahara's moves and countering with quick moves of his own, trying to catch the other man off balance.

As Christopher watched, he began to see the match as symbolic of a different struggle. Nakahara—strong, purposeful, disciplined—seemed to personify Japan. Like Nakahara, the Japanese economy was powerful and highly regimented. It was the reigning champion, and seemingly invincible. The United States, Christopher thought, was like Amaratsu: formerly dominant but no longer the best, and trying to regain its form. And like Amaratsu, the United States was not known for its order and regimentation, but had succeeded thanks to its resourcefulness, its innovation, and its capacity to adapt. Christopher leaned forward in his chair, absorbed in the sumo match and the greater significance it had now taken on for him.

Nakahara and Amaratsu continued to grapple, but the champion still found it impossible to defeat his opponent by applying superior force. Amaratsu remained elusive and cagey. Then, in a flash, Amaratsu feinted in one direction and drove forward toward his opponent's midsection, thrusting with his shoulder while grabbing for Nakahara's legs. The move was quick and unexpected, and Nakahara toppled backwards, landing solidly on his rear. The judge signaled the match even at one round apiece and the crowd burst into a sudden and loud ovation.

"What a reversal!" Christopher exclaimed. "That was quite a move."

"Remarkable!" cried Ken.

The crowd soon fell silent as the warriors paused and prepared for the final and deciding round. Nakahara huddled with his aides, talking calmly but seriously and planning for the final round. It reminded Christopher of a production crew making sure that parts would be built according to schedule.

Amaratsu stood off by himself, speaking to no one, twitching nervously.

"Ah, now comes the final match," said Ken, also excited by the tension and drama of the contest. "Let us see who will prevail."

Again Nakahara and Amaratsu drove toward each other, colliding massively in the center of the *dohyo*. And once again, Amaratsu moved quickly and evasively, not allowing himself to be overwhelmed by the champion's greater strength. Nakahara, meanwhile, was frustrated by Amaratsu's tactics but unable to change his style; he seemed to know just one way to wrestle, and Amaratsu refused to fight him on those terms. The third and deciding round continued for a good spell, and the drama built to a peak. Neither man seemed able to defeat the other. Then, as the crowd watched with amazement, Amaratsu again lunged for his opponent's legs, grasped them perfectly with his arms, and then thrust his weight upwards, gaining leverage and flipping Nakahara over on his side. Nakahara's giant body landed on the ground with a loud thud that shook the *dohyo* and echoed throughout the arena.

With a wave from his fan, the *gyoji* signaled that the match was over—and Amaratsu was once again the champion of sumo.

The crowd was on its feet, applauding wildly. Bewildered, but still acting in accordance with sumo tradition, Nakahara bowed and walked slowly from the ring. His disciplined style, so successful for the past few years, had been defeated by an experienced but agile and clever opponent. Amaratsu smiled broadly and showed a spontaneous joy.

Christopher also smiled as the match ended, happy with the victory of the underdog, pleased that the old master had summoned the will and nerve to defeat his former student.

Perhaps there was a message for America in this contest, Christopher thought. In recent years, Americans had spent a lot of time and energy trying to become like the Japanese. Maybe they needed to try a different approach. Maybe America, like Amaratsu, would do better to concentrate on what it did best.

Chapter 9

Christopher awoke the next morning feeling rested and calm. The sun's rays streamed through the curtains and cast a pattern of light across the carpet, extending from the windows to the foot of the bed. Christopher glanced at his watch and saw that it was already 9 A.M. Slowly, he rolled out of bed and walked across the room to gaze out the window.

It was a clear Sunday morning, a bright spring day that reminded him of pleasant Sundays at home. Tokyo looked vast but quiet, with clusters of skyscrapers spread out across the horizon. Due east, standing out sharply against the morning sun, was the central district, with the Imperial Palace and Ginza not far beyond. The city looked tranquil in the bright sunshine.

Christopher washed and dressed, then slowly made his way to the restaurant near the lobby. After eating, he had a second cup of coffee and leaned back in his chair.

Sunday was a free day, a day without a planned itinerary, a chance to pause from the dizzying activities and tours that had occupied him since his arrival in Japan. It was also, Christopher noted, the fourth day of his journey. Only two days remained before he was scheduled to fly back to America and deliver his report to the management of the Covenant Corporation.

What would he tell them? What would he say about adopting Japanese ways of business management and production? Like many Americans, executives at the Covenant Corporation believed that the restoration of American economic health could be found in Japanese techniques and practices. And

Christopher used to share that view. But after seeing the Japanese economy up close, he had become skeptical.

Getting up from the table, Christopher returned to his room and gathered his notes and clipboard, placing them in his briefcase. I need to spend some time thinking about my mission, he said to himself. I need to gain some perspective and decide what I have to do next.

Deciding to find a quiet spot in a park to reflect and think, Christopher reached for his briefcase and returned to street level, where he took a taxicab to Ueno Park. It was, as Ken had said, a beautiful park, built upon a hilltop, and covered with blossoming cherry trees. The grounds were immaculately tended and clean. Japanese of all ages strolled through the park, visiting the museums and shrines, enjoying the fresh spring day. It was a perfect place to sit and think.

Christopher found a bench at the edge of Shinobazu Pond and sat down.

Placing his briefcase next to him on the bench, he popped open the lid and removed a stack of notes and a pad of blank paper. Carefully, often stopping to reflect, he read the notes he had taken while preparing for his trip to Japan. They spoke glowingly of Japanese achievement, efficiency, and progress. His reviews of recent best-sellers, like *Theory Z*, gushed with admiration for the loyalty and harmony that supposedly typified Japanese industry, and presented the educational system in a wonderful light. Other notes contrasted the success of Japanese industry with the recent troubles of American business. Christopher saw his notes from the NBC White Paper with its catchy title, " If Japan Can, Why Can't We?" He had carefully quoted the narrator, Lloyd Dobyns: "Unless we solve the problems of productivity, our children will be the first generation of Americans to live worse than their parents."

Christopher sighed. All of these notes urged the same thing—adoption of Japanese methods by American business. Dobyns had phrased the idea in its starkest terms: adapt or die. This exhortation had once made sense to Christopher, but now it seemed naive and simplistic. Improving productivity was one thing; becoming like the Japanese was a different matter.

In the first place, thought Christopher, Japan was not the land of progress and prosperity he had imagined. As he had seen, and as Ken had explained, rates of economic growth and GNP didn't adequately describe how the Japanese lived. The lot of the average Japanese citizen wasn't better than that of the average American.

And although clearly successful, Japanese industry didn't exemplify the trust and dignity that he had been led to expect. Christopher had seen enough pressure and coerced loyalty to convince him that the popular portrayal of Japanese business was idyllic. There were, he recognized, several areas where the Covenant Corporation could learn from the Japanese, but in general it didn't provide the shining example that American best-sellers had led him to expect.

Christopher again let out a deep sigh and put his notes in his lap.

A mild breeze rippled through the park and the cherry blossoms fluttered gently. Families and couples walked by. The pond shimmered before him.

So what am I going to do? Christopher wondered. What am I going to recommend? What can I tell Ridgeman and the others back at the Covenant Corporation? I can't go back and tell them that we should become just like the Japanese. But what am I going to suggest instead?

Christopher's thoughts were interrupted by a faint noise of footsteps in the distance. Looking up, he could see a pair of runners approaching on a footpath. Soon several more came into view, and then many more. Christopher stood up and walked over to the path. Each runner wore a shirt, shorts, and a cap identifying his company affiliation. It was, Christopher realized, a company organized race, with employees spending their one day off running together, demonstrating unity and loyalty and all those other qualities that Japanese firms demanded of their employees.

The stream of joggers flowed by, endlessly. What most impressed Christopher was their concentration: they gazed ahead and straight downward, and their angled, bobbing elbows seemed to move synchronously. It reminded him of the total orchestration of body movements he had seen at the Toshima Motor Company—*fit*, *weld*, *bolt*, *test*. He moved closer to them. They did not lift their eyes or change course, but continued running, moving as if part of a large herd.

As he observed the runners, who seemed oblivious to his presence, a line of poetry he had read somewhere surfaced in his consciousness:

> *Unreal City.* . . .
> *A crowd flowed over London Bridge, so many,*
> *I had not thought death had undone so many.*
> *Sighs, short and infrequent, were exhaled,*
> *And each man fixed his eyes before his feet.*

Unreal City—that was Tokyo all right. Things ran too well here; everything was organized and structured. And that was the problem. Only rare individuals, like Ken Yusi, possessed the fortitude to reject the pressure to conform. The lesson is clear, Christopher thought. Unless a society makes some effort to preserve the sanctity of the individual it will soon turn into a giant machine, its people reduced to cogs and gears, grinding soulessly away. And the machine, lacking the resistance provided by free-thinking individuals, would turn faster and faster until it flew apart, ironically destroyed by its own success.

Christopher returned to the bench and looked back at the joggers. Nothing had changed. He couldn't tell if these were new joggers, or the same ones. For all he knew they could have been running in a large circle. Christopher picked up his notes and reached to put them back in his briefcase. Suddenly, something caught his eye. It was the small package Mark

Truitt had given him before he left the United States. Unwrapping the package, Christopher found a book. He turned it over in his hand and read the title: *Selected Prose and Poetry of Ralph Waldo Emerson*. How strange. Why would Mark give me a copy of Emerson? He opened the book and found an inscription: "You can find green grass in your own backyard. You don't have to go over the hill for it. Mark." Christopher smiled. Typically cryptic, he thought. But why send it with me to Japan? He leafed through the book and noted that Mark had highlighted some passages. Christopher began reading.

The first essay, "Self-Reliance," had an epigram in Latin—*Ne te quaesiveris extra*—which Mark had translated as "Do not seek yourself outside yourself." What exactly did Mark have in mind? Christopher began working through Emerson's prose. Each sentence was clear and precise.

> *Every man has his own voice, manner, eloquence, and, just as much, his own sort of . . . imagination and action. Let him scorn to imitate any being, let him scorn to be a secondary man.*

As he pondered this advice, Christopher glanced back at the continuing stream of joggers, who filed by in cookie-cutter sameness. He returned to Emerson:

> *Whoso would be a man, must be a nonconformist . . . Nothing is at last sacred but the integrity of your own mind . . . imitation is suicide.*

These were basic tenets of American thought, Christopher realized. These ideas, stressing individuality and freedom, were values that had helped make America great. They had inspired invention and ingenuity; they had fostered creativity and progress. And little had changed since Emerson had written these words in the 1840s—they were as instructive today as they were then. Christopher read on:

> *A foolish consistency is the hobgoblin of little minds.*

That's it, Christopher said to himself, taking a short breath. That's the problem with the Japanese method—its emphasis on conformity, or in Emerson's words, "consistency," was taken to foolish and destructive lengths. At the Nakano Electrical Company, for example, the *kanban* system had been taken to an unhealthy extreme. Of course, any organization had to be consistent, but at the same time it had to allow for the occasional deviation, the exception to the rule, the free play necessary for growth and development. In America, order was intended to encourage freedom, not conformity. That was where the Japanese system failed—it didn't permit free play, it didn't allow for deviation. And this rigorous conformity stifled imagination and freedom of expression.

"Trust thyself," Emerson admonished. "Every heart vibrates to that iron string." Yet how few in Japan could assert that individuality. How different from America! In America, the individual was considered superior to the group; in America, the individual could help change the system. Christopher smiled at his own blindness. What a joke to seek a solution to our problems in Japan, he thought. Japan is the most perfect cultural opposite America could find.

It was now becoming clear: the solution to American problems lay not in Japan, but in America. Rather than imitate others, America needed to return to its traditional values of self-reliance and individuality, values that had served it well throughout its history. Christopher thought back to the sumo match of the night before—Amaratsu hadn't won by imitating or changing his style, but had relied on his individual qualities and strengths. And so it would have to be with America.

So what am I doing here? Christopher asked himself. Why was I sent to Japan? Emerson had already answered this. A man travels, Emerson wrote, "when his necessities, his duties, on any occasion call him from his house, or into foreign lands," but he should visit "like a sovereign and not like an interloper or valet." The "wise man stays at home," not physically, but culturally and spiritually. Valet—the word stuck in Christopher's mind. He swallowed. What had he been but a valet, a sycophant of the Japanese? And what was America, looking overseas for a solution to her problems, but a lackey of the quick-fix, the instant remedy? His mission, Christopher realized, was itself a form of imitation, motivated by a naive belief that the solution to a problem always lies somewhere else and not with ourselves. Instead, Emerson maintained, a man should look into himself, at what he called Intuition, the "primary wisdom" in which "all things find their common origin." Yes, Christopher concurred, closing his eyes and leaning back against the bench. Emerson counseled a sensitivity to one's own instincts and intuitions, which Christopher had felt but had been unable to articulate or even truly understand until he had met Yusi. He had ignored his intuition when he had repressed doubts about the school system, about the factory regimentation, and about Mr. Sakatumi's sterile family life.

It was all pretty obvious now. America could learn a few things from the Japanese, but overall, when it came to essential questions, it had to improve its situation on its own, in its own terms.

Christopher thought back to Mark's inscription. Now I understand it, he reflected. The grass always looks greener on the other side of the hill, but it seldom is. Mark knew all along that I wouldn't find any secret of Japanese productivity—at least, no magical secret that I could transplant to America. But like a good teacher, he let me find out for myself, rather than tell me the answer. And it's a lesson I won't forget easily. Christopher thought of Ridgeman and Lagrange. I'll have to explain this in my report—they'll certainly want to know if we've been heading in the wrong direction.

The joggers continued past, eyes fixed in front, arms moving in coordination. Yes, this was an overorganized society, even dehumanizing at times, but there were things to be learned from the Japanese as well—the spirit of cooperation; the conscientious devotion to the needs of the customer; and yes, the inescapable fact that men did live in groups, that the individual sometimes had to yield. There seemed to be a natural conflict between the group and individual, Christopher thought. What would Emerson say about that? He turned to the later essays. "If there are conflicting evidences," read one highlighted passage, "why not state them? . . . The philosophy we want is one of fluxion and mobility." Christopher smiled. Emerson was stressing the need for a pragmatic balance, an open and flexible approach, rather than a "foolish consistency." What Mark, and what Emerson before him, were trying to say was, *don't oversimplify, keep an open mind, but be skeptical and pragmatic. You may learn a few things from others, but in the end you will only learn from yourself.* "That's my lesson, all right," Christopher said out loud. "It's the Covenant Corporation's lesson, and it's America's lesson as well."

He thought of Hornblower and Faithful, Americans who represented opposite attitudes toward the Japanese. Hornblower was too individualistic and resentful, unwilling to deal with facts, complications, or necessities; and Faithful was too much of a follower, blind to his own impulses and instincts, naive, afraid to listen to his own drummer. Neither attitude was finally acceptable. Neither way would provide an answer for America. The only way was the middle way—which meant knowing when to adopt the appropriate attitude, when to restrict, when to relax. This was real thought—not remaining secure in static ideas, but dynamically interacting with ideas and reality, what Emerson called "*man thinking.*" "So far as a man thinks, he is free," said Emerson. And like freedom, thinking involved the continual reconciliation of opposites— such as balancing the needs of the individual against the demands of the society, each to the benefit of the other.

Suddenly Christopher heard giggling from the far end of the clearing. There were several adolescents, each carrying a pack and conventionally dressed in school blazers. They called out greetings to their friends, who were coming to join them. Christopher looked at his watch. It was 3 P.M. exactly. The teenagers were gathering for some reason, and with the usual

Japanese punctuality. Behind him Christopher could hear the joggers in their endless procession. He watched as the adolescents pulled large portable stereos from their satchels and changed into clothes of bright, clashing colors. Some wore different colored sneakers, pants legs of different lengths, outrageous earrings clamped to the nose, tank tops with chains wrapped around them. A few girls wore patent leather vests, usually black, extra high heels, tight leather pants, and had "tatoos" applied to their arms with felt pens.

Christopher was fascinated., He had not expected to find punk rockers in Japan. Were they perhaps, in their adolescent way, rebelling against the conformity of Japanese society? Western rock music came on loud and incessant, flooding the park. "I want to be anarchy," snarled the lead singer in English. The Japanese kids imitated him as best they could, and began to dance—or something, Christopher couldn't quite say. They donned roller skates and gyrated like dervishes, they jumped up and down in pogo fashion, they rolled on the ground, they screamed incongruously and made faces, they laughed uproariously, giddily, unpredictably. The energy was incredible, but so was the disorganization. Maybe this, in a crude and inarticulate form, was the Emersonian individual trying to break free. Christopher looked behind him. The joggers ran on, mechanically, mindlessly. He looked back at the teenagers, dancing chaotically.

Christopher watched for a while. Suddenly, the music went off. One by one, the punk rockers changed back into their conventional clothes. School blazers replaced leather vests and tank tops. "Tatoos" were removed. Young ladies became modest and demure, young men silent and well dressed. Almost on cue, the kids, now looking more like preppies, or tomorrow's Chamber of Commerce, went their separate ways. Christopher looked at his watch. Four P.M. Recess is over, he thought, chagrined. It wasn't hard to see what had happened. These teenagers, these innocent exemplars of youthful individuality and self-expression, were already contained within

the system and didn't know it. By allowing a measure of re-
bellion on Sunday afternoon, the society prevented it from
turning into genuine social dissent. This was how Japan
avoided creating people like Yusi—real individuals. Christopher felt a surge of admiration for Ken's moral courage and
fortitude. He hadn't given in, and he hadn't left. If Emerson
wanted a disciple, Christopher thought, he couldn't do better
than Ken Yusi.

Heartened by his new understanding, Christopher wondered whether he, too, could strike the balance represented by
Yusi and articulated by Emerson and Truitt. One way to start,
he concluded, is to ask some hard questions when I visit the
factory tomorrow. He gathered his book and briefcase, nodded
good-bye to the silent, oblivious parade of joggers, and made
his way out of the park.

Chapter 10

Mr. Sakatumi did not have to ring for Christopher the next day; the American was waiting at the curb when the Wanasumi Company car drew alongside. The door swung open and Christopher slid into the backseat.

"Good morning, Mr. Newman," said Mr. Sakatumi in a neutral tone. "I hope you are feeling better today."

"Feeling better?" Christopher was puzzled. "But I wasn't sick."

"Oh," said Mr. Sakatumi. He seemed confused. "You did not continue tour even though you were well?" he asked tentatively.

"That's right," Christopher replied. "I just wanted some time to myself, that's all."

"Ah, that is not Japanese way," Mr. Sakatumi said, bowing his head slightly. Christopher once again felt an indirect disapproval in Mr. Sakatumi's seemingly polite rejoinder.

After a brief, uncomfortable silence, Christopher said, "Well, I'm not Japanese. In America, if we need a day off to relax, we take it. We know that if we take too many days off we could lose our jobs, so we're careful not to overdo it. It's a matter of trust between employer and employee."

"Unfortunately, that policy could disrupt production," replied Mr. Sakatumi. He did not look at Christopher as he spoke.

Christopher sighed. "Yes, but what good is production if it reduces the worker to an automaton? After all, who are we producing for? In America, we like to let people know what their responsibilities are, then let them make their choices freely. Ideally, we seek a balance between cooperation and freedom."

Christopher looked out the window. It was the same story, repeated one more time: subordination of the individual to the group; order valued above freedom. He felt a little impatient with Mr. Sakatumi.

"Today you will see example of improvement in production efficiency," Mr. Sakatumi continued evenly. "We are returning to Toshima Motor Company, to show example of productivity gain."

"Do you think we could visit a research and development lab instead?" asked Christopher. "I'm interested in Japanese research and innovation, and I've already seen two manufacturing plants."

"Itinerary says we are to visit factory, Mr. Newman. Besides, most R&D work is in special labs, and not available to visitors. I think is best to visit factories."

"Well, I'm very curious about your R&D efforts. I've seen a lot of emphasis on production, but little on invention or creativity."

"Oh, Japanese R&D very good," Mr. Sakatumi said in a matter-of-fact tone.

Christopher smiled to himself. Is that why Hitachi pirated IBM's design for semiconductor devices? he wondered. Is that why a Swiss watchmaker won compensation from Seiko for copying machine tool technology? The truth, he now understood, was that the Japanese strength in productivity was largely due to traits of obedience, order, and regimentation, and these same traits were obstacles to the innovation necessary for original design and invention. The entire Japanese way—which emphasized memorization in school, repetition in work and sports, and obedience rather than individuality—was an impediment to creativity. No wonder the Japanese were good imitators but poor inventors.

The car slowed suddenly as it approached the factory.

Christopher waited for Mr. Sakatumi to continue talking about Japanese R&D. No comments were forthcoming.

The limousine slowed at the TMC gates. Mr. Sakatumi showed the guard his guest pass and they proceeded to the main entrance. He escorted Christopher through the steel doors and onto the production floor, where Mr. Suzuki was waiting. He smiled broadly as they approached and bowed to his guests.

"I will return at eleven fifty-five for lunch," said Mr. Sakatumi, who bowed and left.

Mr. Suzuki turned excitedly to Christopher. "Newman-san, most wonderful thing has happened."

"Really?" said Christopher curiously.

"Oh, yes!" said Mr. Suzuki. "I must show you."

They walked to a nearby production line, where workers were assembling rear bumpers to auto bodies. It was the same team of workers Christopher had observed a few days earlier. The men wore the same blue jumpsuits, black sneakers, and caps with the TMC insignia, and they moved in the same rapid, coordinated manner.

"They're as efficient as ever," Christopher observed.

"Ah, team is *much* more productive than before," smiled Mr. Suzuki. "This team reduce time to assemble bumper by 5 percent. It is a bright day for TMC."

Christopher looked closer. The workers were really straining. Drops of sweat ran from their foreheads and down their chins, only to be flung off as they went through their programmed motions. Despite the loud noise from the surrounding machinery, Christopher could hear short, quick breaths as the workers exerted themselves. *Fit*, *weld*, *bolt*, *test*—the same rhythm prevailed, but faster. Christopher suddenly remembered the joggers in the park, puffing like miniature steam locomotives.

"So they cut a few seconds off of their time," Christopher said. "Does it really make a big difference? And how do the workers feel about it?"

"Oh, difference is very great," replied Mr. Suzuki gravely. "A 5 percent reduction in bumper assembly time mean we can make forty-five more cars a day. That is 13,500 more cars a year, and a profit increase of—"

"Thanks, I get the picture," Christopher said abruptly. "But what about the workers? How do they feel about the speedup?"

"Group is most happy," said Mr. Suzuki. "Group is happy to make more cars for TMC. It is best way to show loyalty to company and contribute to harmony."

Christopher sighed quietly. Obviously, Mr. Suzuki didn't perceive the workers as individuals who might feel uncomfortable with the increased pace. He seemed to think of them only as a group, as a unit of input in the production process. And, Christopher realized, it was useless trying to convince him otherwise. Mr. Suzuki was too conditioned to see things one way. It was as though he and Christopher were looking at the same object and seeing two different things.

As he and Mr. Suzuki left the bumper assembly line, Christopher noticed a worker carrying a ladder and a sign. Mr. Suzuki explained that it was a safety sign. The man positioned the ladder next to an enormous punch press. As the worker began climbing the ladder, safety sign in hand, the punch press suddenly crunched a piece of steel metal, stripping it of excess, and popped it out onto a constantly moving rail, which carried the newly molded section to the next operation.

"I'm glad to see you're concerned about safety," said Christopher. After seeing the strain on the bumper assembly line, he wondered if much thought was given to protecting workers from power bolt drivers and welding torches. He sensed that the frenzied pace of production could lead to fatigue, with serious consequences.

"Safety is most important," said Mr. Suzuki. "Each foreman try to maintain record of group safety. It is best for productivity."

"There's no question the Japanese are productive," Christopher agreed, "but I'm also interested in R&D. What kinds of innovations have you made in your products?"

"TMC take special pride in R&D," said Mr. Suzuki. "It help make production more efficient. For instance, we perfect fuel injection for automobiles so they not need smog equipment for U.S. Also, we put microprocessor in our biggest model car, so driver know when he need gas." Mr. Suzuki smiled proudly.

"But those aren't achievements of TMC," Christopher countered. "Fuel injection was available in Volkswagens in the late sixties. And the microprocessor you use was designed in America." As Christopher recalled, the only radical new design the Japanese had introduced was the Wankel engine— itself the invention of a German engineer—and that was a disaster. Not only did it get poor gas mileage, it also leaked oil and ran erratically.

Mr. Suzuki appeared offended by Christopher's remark. It was the same look of guilt Christopher had often seen in Japan. He saw that Japanese society maintained control of its citizens by instituting a deep sense of guilt or shame, and thereby conditioned behavior. And Japanese companies had merely refined the technique. Many cultures rely on guilt and shame, he said to himself, but not to the extent of the Japanese.

"We have very good quality control," said Mr. Suzuki, in a flat voice, trying to change the subject.

"Yes, but where did those ideas of quality control come from? They came from America—Juran, Cummings, and Deming," Christopher responded. "Japan put their ideas in practice, and perhaps refined them, but it really didn't invent or originate anything."

At that very moment, a "just-in-time" delivery truck screeched to a stop in front of them. Christopher noticed that the driver, like the bumper assemblers, looked strained and agitated.

"See. 'Just-in-time' delivery system work very well," said Mr. Suzuki. The driver took the small box out of the otherwise empty truck bed and handed it quickly to a line worker. He then jumped back in the truck and drove away.

"It is true, R&D not best in Japan," conceded Mr. Suzuki, "but production efficiency and inventory management very good."

Christopher noticed that the employee with the safety sign had reached the top of the ladder and was about to place the sign on the punch press.

He turned to Mr. Suzuki. "I have a question for you. I agree that R&D isn't a strength of yours. And Japan doesn't have many natural resources, either. How long do you think you can live off production alone? The Koreans are already more efficient at steel—they can make it better and cheaper, because their labor costs are lower. If Japan doesn't invent new products or technologies, and its one great strength, production, is already being undercut, what is going to happen? Isn't Japan going to be very vulnerable in coming years?"

"Yes," said Mr. Suzuki, "but we still take better care of our people—"

Just then the punch press slammed shut on another piece of sheet metal. The vibrations shook the ladder, and the worker, unable to keep his balance, fell backwards into the machine, the sign flying in the opposite direction. The worker, stunned by the fall, could not move quickly enough, and as the machine opened, it crushed his hand and wrist. A scream pierced the plant and the foreman came running, shouting. The production line suddenly stopped.

Two workers descended into the punch press and extricated the fallen man, whose screams continued to echo through the building. The foreman barked some orders and the two workers shoved a towel in the injured man's mouth. The man was pale, and his eyes rolled in his head. The rescue workers strapped him to the stretcher brought by the foreman. As they carried the man up out of the machine, Christopher saw what was left of his hand and arm. He breathed deeply to control the sick feeling rising within him. The workers placed the stretcher on a "just-in-time" delivery truck and began to swath the arm in gauze. The worker's muffled screams grew fainter, turned into moans, and stopped altogether as he lost consciousness.

"Where's the ambulance?" asked Christopher, turning to Mr. Suzuki.

"Oh, 'just-in-time' delivery truck is much faster," said Mr. Suzuki in a neutral voice. As the truck sped off, other employees rushed up to the foreman, who was obviously upset.

"The foreman is very concerned," said Christopher. "I'm glad to see that."

"Yes, foreman is concerned about all his employees. Also he had a spotless safety record," replied Mr. Suzuki. "But now it is ruined. It is great shame. He is accepting apologies from other workers. They make promise not to stop production line again."

"What? Do you mean—" Christopher's response was cut short by the sudden crunching of the press. The injured man hadn't been gone twenty seconds, and the machine was working again. As the molded metal popped out onto the conveyor belt, Christopher remembered a comment Mr. Suzuki made during his first visit at TMC: "Production line never stop." He looked at the foreman, who rushed over to an older man, obviously a manager, and bowed deeply. The manager said a few soft words, then barked and pointed at the workers. The foreman grunted in what seemed an ominous tone. The workers disappeared into the line. Everything was as before. Barely a minute had passed.

"Most sorry, Newman-san, for interruption of tour," said Mr. Suzuki. "Shall we go to next part of plant?"

"No, I don't think so," Christopher said quietly. He felt as if he were in a fog. "I think I've had enough."

The punch press slammed again, and Christopher felt the sick feeling return. Harmony, mutual trust, intimacy—all of these wonderful words had dissolved in front of his eyes. Here was the essence of Japanese production management: pressure, shame, and the imperative to produce, produce, produce.

He started for the lobby, and was immediately joined by Mr. Suzuki.

"Guide must always accompany visitor," Mr. Suzuki said politely. Christopher said nothing, but headed for the lobby, where he found Mr. Sakatumi waiting.

"I'd like to go back to the hotel," Christopher said firmly.

"But itinerary say tour must last until eleven fifty-five," Mr. Sakatumi answered.

"I don't care what the itinerary says," Christopher snapped. "Where's the car?"

Mr. Sakatumi and Mr. Suzuki bowed to one another. Christopher, impatient to leave, simply walked out of the lobby by himself. On the way to the gate, he passed the Japanese rock garden. It was as immaculate as ever, with not a stone out of place. But now it seemed barren and hard—not at all life-enhancing, but rigid and dead. Rock garden, assembly line, school, family, even sports—it was all the same. Christopher felt weary. Out on the street he hailed a taxi, and returned to the hotel.

When he got to his room, Christopher packed and made several phone calls. He reserved a flight home that evening on Pan Am, then called Ken Yusi to tell him he was leaving. Yusi was out, so he left a message with the secretary promising that he would soon be in touch. He then called Mr. Sakatumi's answering machine and thanked him for his hospitality. Reaching for his suitcase, Christopher headed for the lobby, where he took the next limousine for the airport, feeling disappointed but relieved.

Chapter 11

The trip back to America was long and uneventful, and it gave Christopher a chance to recover from the shock of the factory accident. He found the solitude of the nearly empty plane a source of solace, enabling him to reflect on his experiences in Japan. Finally, the plane began its final descent, and Christopher, tired but happy to be home again, prepared for the landing. Once at the gate, he seized his briefcase and jacket and walked out into the terminal, where Nancy was waiting for him. They passed through the baggage claim area and drove home.

Sarah was asleep when they arrived, but awoke shortly after dinner. Christopher played with her for a while, then put her to bed. As he closed the door to Sarah's room, he thought of Mrs. Sakatumi with a child on her back, bending over her older son in their tiny bedroom, supervising his homework. Suddenly, as he walked back to the living room, Christopher realized how big his house was—a mansion compared to Mr. Sakatumi's cramped apartment. Even the drive home from the airport, now that he thought of it, was smooth and easy, the traffic sparse, the roads wide. The differences between Japan and America were palpable—and it was Christopher's job to communicate that to the Covenant Corporation. He went to sleep that night pondering how best to present his findings.

The next morning he called headquarters and asked the switchboard to connect him with Franklin Ridgeman.

A few seconds later Ridgeman's voice came on the line.

"Newman? Is that you?"

"Hello, Mr. Ridgeman. I'm calling to let you know I'm back from Japan. I arrived last night."

"Excellent! I trust you cracked the code?"

"Yes, I guess I did, sir," Christopher replied. "I learned a lot."

"Good, good. Well, we're all looking forward to your report. I'm going to call a special executive manager's meeting for 9 A.M. this Thursday. How does that sound?"

"It sounds fine," said Christopher, feeling a bit apprehensive. He noted he had just forty-eight hours to put his presentation together.

"Great. We'll see you then," Ridgeman said. Then he added: "I knew you'd come through."

Before Christopher could thank him, Ridgeman hung up. Christopher thought for a moment, then placed a call to Mark Truitt at the local college.

"How was the trip?" Mark asked.

"Well, I'd like to talk to you about it. Can we have lunch today?"

"Sure," Mark said. "I know a little place near the campus. I think you'll like it "

Mark was in his office when Christopher arrived at the college. They passed through a basement corridor and up a flight of stairs, then emerged into tne bright sunshine of the spring day. The weather was pleasant and clear, and the contours of the campus were sharply defined against the background of the blue sky. The bells of the clock tower rang in harmony to announce the noon hour.

"So how was your journey?" asked Mark with a smile as they walked across the campus.

"I went to Japan to learn," said Christopher wryly, "but the lessons were a little different from what I expected."

"That's not surprising," said Mark sympathetically.

Christopher smiled, a little embarrassed, but happy that Mark avoided taking a superior attitude. Then he continued in a slow and deliberate voice.

"Japan was pretty impressive. People were friendly, and Tokyo was safe. I was never worried about walking alone at night. Some of their business practices are excellent, and I'll tell Covenant all about them. But what really sticks in my mind is the difference between America and Japan—and how their culture determines, down to the smallest detail, how they do business."

Mark nodded, then gestured. "Here we are."

They entered a small, dark, tavernlike restaurant and bar. At one end were some windows with a door opening onto a patio. Customers were scattered throughout the room, some drinking mugs of beer, others eating sandwiches. There were students, some professors, construction workers, office workers, and a hobo sitting off by himself.

Rock music from a jukebox filled the restaurant. Christopher and Mark passed through the serving line and ordered sandwiches, then walked out to the patio, choosing a quiet table away from the lunch crowd. From their table they could see the campus across the street, looking calm and peaceful.

"Tell me," said Mark, cutting his sandwich in half, "were the Japanese as cooperative as they're said to be? That's supposed to be their trademark."

"They may be cooperative," Christopher replied, "but behind the facade of harmony there's terrific pressure to conform. Americans wouldn't buy that—they're too independent. The Japanese talk about loyalty, but it's an imposed loyalty, a matter of necessity, not choice. The same goes for guaranteed employment—it's not what it appears to be."

"That figures," Mark observed. "Appearance and reality are not always the same thing."

He paused for a moment, then continued.

"Say, have you ever read Twain or James?"

"Well, I think I did in college," Christopher replied.

"One of their major themes—and this is particularly true for James—is the innocence and gullibility of Americans abroad, and how older cultures can take advantage of that innocence. You see the same gullibility in our weakness for fads—like thinking the Japanese have found the 'secret' of business success. It's something we have to guard against."

"Well," said Christopher, "that was certainly true in my case. I learned, though."

"Good," Mark said. "But a sign of wisdom is recognizing what you don't have to know. That's where the Covenant Corporation and I parted company. I told them not to bother imitating the Japanese, to spend more time improving our own way of doing things, and they demoted me."

Christopher nodded softly.

A stout man with short gray hair and an apron emerged from the restaurant with a pot of coffee in his hand.

"That's Heinz," said Mark. "He's the owner, and a real nice man. He's run this place ever since he came over from Germany, thirty years ago."

Heinz walked over to the table.

"Hallo, Mark. Vud you like coffee?"

"Sure," said Mark, holding out his cup. "How's everything?"

Heinz poured the coffee and shrugged. "Ach, not so goot. I had a couple of loud fellows here last night. You know, dey drink too much beer and make trouble and scare de udder customers."

"Oh, yeah?" Mark asked. "What happened?"

"Ja, vell. I call de Polizei," Heinz shrugged again. "But vat can I do? Dose crazy guys come here and make trouble, zo I have to do someding about it."

"I hope they get the message," Mark said.

"Ja, me too," said Heinz. He excused himself and turned to the next table.

Christopher looked over at Mark. "That's too bad about the rowdiness."

"Unfortunately, that's what we have to put up with in a free society. It's the old problem: how do you balance one guy's freedom to get drunk with someone else's right to peace and quiet? Where do you draw the line between individual liberty and the need for order?"

Christopher nodded. "I know. It's a problem. I don't like rowdies, but I'd rather put up with them occasionally than feel suffocated like I did in Japan. That was constant—and unbearable."

"Yeah," Mark agreed, "And besides, in the long run, isn't freedom—to live as one wants, to choose, to create—isn't that what drives an economy, a nation? It was Apple, not IBM, that introduced the personal computer. Two guys in a garage, not an anonymous corporation."

"I wonder if those guys read Emerson," Christopher said with a laugh.

"I kind of doubt it," Mark replied, smiling.

They left the restaurant and walked along the street toward the campus. At the corner they came across an ice cream vendor seated in a folding chair next to his cart.

"Care for a dessert?" Christopher asked his friend.

"Sounds good," said Mark.

The vendor stood up as they approached. He wore a V-necked shirt, a white apron over blue jeans, and tennis shoes.

"Two, please," said Christopher, handing the man a dollar bill.

The vendor reached into his cart and pulled out a couple of ice cream bars.

"There you go," he said, handing him the bars and his change. "Thanks."

Mark and Christopher paused momentarily to unwrap the Eskimo Pies.

"How's business?" Mark asked.

"Pretty fair," said the vendor. "I'll be happy when it gets a little warmer. Summer months are always the best."

"Sold ice cream for very long?" asked Christopher.

"Five years now," the vendor answered. "I spent eighteen years as an insurance underwriter, and I got real tired of it.

You know, nine to five, suit and tie, impress the boss. Who needs it? So now I sell ice cream."

"And are you happy with it?" asked Mark.

"For the most part. I like being my own boss. But sometimes business is slow, and sometimes it rains and I get soaked. So I take my chances. But it's my business, and I don't have to apologize to anyone when business is bad."

Christopher suddenly remembered Ridgeman placating Lynch.

"And," the vendor concluded, "I don't have to wear a suit and tie."

Christopher smiled. "Let's hope for a warm summer," he said.

"Yes, sir," said the vendor.

"So long," said Mark as they began their walk back to the campus. Soon they reached the History department.

"When's your presentation?" Mark asked, stopping and turning toward his friend.

"The day after tomorrow," Christopher replied.

"What kind of response do you think you'll get?"

Christopher thought for a moment, then said, "Oh, the executive management committee will be surprised, but they'll recognize the truth in what I tell them."

He paused briefly. "They want to do what's best for company," he added.

"Good," said Mark. "I'm glad to hear that."

Chapter 12

Christopher spent the next two days preparing his presentation to the Covenant Corporation executive committee. He chose to work at home, preferring the quiet and solitude of his study to the activity and interruptions of the office. Christopher pored over his notes, read recent articles about American business, and gradually formulated a set of suggestions and recommendations for the company to follow.

The morning of the meeting was overcast, with clouds hanging motionlessly over the financial district. Christopher parked his car and walked through the skyscraper's tall glass doors, then rode the elevator up to the Executive Suite. The reception area, with its modular furniture and sleek design, was already busy and full of people. No doubt they were executives gathered for the special meeting.

Christopher could hear loud conversation coming from the conference room. As he entered, Franklin Ridgeman approached him, hand extended.

"Welcome back," he said. "Hope the mission went well."

Christopher smiled and shook his hand. Other executives greeted him and began taking their seats.

"We've all been looking forward to this, Newman," Covenant's president said, "and I expect that your recommendations to make the Covenant Corporation as productive as a Japanese firm are going to make you a very important man. You're going to help turn this company around, Newman—and Mr. Lynch will be pleased."

Christopher fidgeted. "Well, I appreciate your confidence,"

he said uncomfortably, "but I think you should hear my presentation before you reach any conclusions."

"Oh, I'm sure you did a fine job." Ridgeman smiled. "Shall we begin?"

Ridgeman called the meeting to order. Christopher was formally introduced and walked to the speaker's stand, where he set down his papers and looked out at the audience. He could see Robert Lagrange and Morton Merriweather, as well as several other highly ranked corporate officers whom he knew by sight but had never met. Most of the audience was quiet and ready to listen.

Christopher began his presentation.

"I'm happy to be here this morning to present my findings from my trip to Japan. It was an interesting week, and a very enlightening one. I learned quite a bit about Japan and also about America, and I believe that the recommendations I will submit to you this morning can help improve the Covenant Corporation's productivity.

"Let me begin by describing how my assignment came about. I was reminded of how strong the Japanese have become, how they've taken the lead in productivity and efficiency, and how several of Covenant's divisions have been hurt by Japanese competition. My mission was simple: learn how to make the Covenant Corporation more like a Japanese company, and thereby restore its health. I was asked to isolate the reasons—the 'secrets'—for Japanese success in business, and bring them home to America."

Several executives nodded as Christopher reviewed the purpose of his mission. Ridgeman looked around the room proudly.

Christopher paused. He grasped the speaker's stand with both hands and looked around the table. He cleared his throat and spoke firmly.

"Ladies and gentlemen, there are no 'secrets' of Japanese management that can magically restore health to American companies. It's not that simple. I discovered that the principles of Japanese management are interwoven with Japanese culture and society; in fact, they are reflections of each other. What underlies Japanese management policies is a complex set of values and customs that have evolved over thousands of years, and that are shaped by geography, climate, language, and religion. We can't simply take a given aspect of Japanese management, even if it looks attractive, and transplant it to the United States with equal results. We can't do that because Japan and America differ enormously in their values, their social structure, and their cultures."

There was a stirring around the table. Members of the audience whispered to each other and looked confused. Some of the smiles had vanished. A man in the back of the room slowly raised his hand.

"Are you telling us that we can't learn from the Japanese?" he asked.

"No," said Christopher in a firm voice. "I'm not saying that we can't learn from the Japanese." This was a critical point, and he wanted to explain his answer clearly. "There are several things that we can learn from them. We can place more emphasis on customer satisfaction, we can learn to develop better lines of supply and delivery, and we can learn to improve inventory management. I've made a special report of these recommendations and I have copies here to distribute to each of you. But these are specific methods. In a larger sense, when considering the overall nature of Japanese business and industry, we are neither able to 'adopt' their ways, nor do I believe that we should want to. Much of their approach to management rests on ideas and values that run counter to our own."

The audience sat silent. Christopher continued.

"Let me give you a few examples. We've all heard about 'guaranteed lifetime employment.' This policy is supposed to assure employment and thereby foster loyalty and stability. Well, I learned that only a minority of Japanese firms have any such policy, and that where it exists, 'lifetime employment' only extends to some of the workers. Women, for instance, are often laid off to protect the jobs of male workers. And only rarely are they given managerial positions. I'm sure that Covenant wouldn't care for that. It doesn't fit our personnel policies, and besides, it's against the law."

Christopher noticed Merriweather looking around the table a bit nervously.

"We've also heard about loyalty, trust, and intimacy in Japanese firms. At first glance there seems to be trust and intimacy, but just below the surface Japanese society is fraught with stress, tension, and pressure to conform. One reason there appears to be such unity and agreement is that no one dares to complain, since complaining is considered dishonorable, and can jeopardize a person's career and place in society. And leaving one company to join another—something Americans take for granted—is considered disgraceful and is seldom done. Also the emphasis on seniority makes it difficult to start a new job at equivalent rank and salary. So you see, company loyalty isn't really voluntary."

Christopher paused and looked around the room. Most people looked doubtful, and a few openly shook their heads. Lagrange looked angry; Ridgeman was stunned.

Continuing with his report, Christopher described his visits to TMC and the Nakano Electrical Company, again mentioning some benefits of Japanese inventory management, but warning against the extreme regimentation and absolute conformity demanded of the employees. He talked about the Japanese educational system that taught repetition but not creativity; he mentioned the approach to sports that involved endless practice and squashed individuality. The attention of the audience seemed to rise and set with Christopher's positive and negative observations about the Japanese. Their bewilderment peaked when he argued that Japanese business practices were a reflection of culture and values.

"The Japanese approach to management looks impressive at first glance," he said in summary, "but it runs counter to American values and would never work at the Covenant Corporation. Trying to make our factories like the Japanese isn't the answer."

Suddenly, Lagrange rose from his chair and pointed a finger at Christopher.

"Listen, Newman, I think this has gone about far enough! You've missed the whole point. So what if Japanese business methods run counter to American values and culture? That just means we have to adopt Japanese values as well as their management techniques. If we have to adopt their values to become successful, then that's what we'd better do! Right?"

He glared at Christopher, who returned his gaze.

"Not necessarily," Christopher answered. "First, a nation can't simply change its values the way a man might change his shirt. Values, customs, culture—these are what give a people identity. Japanese values emphasize submission to the group, obedience, honor at all costs—that *is* Japan. But American values stress freedom, individuality, and self-reliance. They encourage cooperation among equals. Our values are our heritage—they're what make America special."

Lagrange continued to stare—a bit more coldly, it seemed. He took a long breath.

"Second," Christopher continued quickly, "are the Japanese really so successful? Productivity and GNP are high, but those are only one measure of an economy. In quality of life, freedom, self-sufficiency, they're no better off than we are. I agree that American industry needs revitalization, but I don't think Japan is the example we should follow."

Lagrange snorted skeptically and sat down. He folded his arms and stared straight ahead, his face showing disgust and irritation.

Christopher stopped momentarily. There was total silence in the room. This was not the reaction he had expected.

Morton Merriweather, Covenant's Director of Personnel, raised his hand and spoke. "Gosh, Chris, I think your observations sound very helpful. I agree that we have to pay attention to the needs and feelings of our employees."

"Aw, shut up, Merriweather!" Lagrange growled. "What do you know, anyway? You're just from Personnel."

Sensing the need to restore order, Franklin Ridgeman rose to his feet.

"Well, Newman," he said, as the other managers turned their attention in his direction, "how *are* we going to fix things if we don't become more like the Japanese, I'd like to know."

Christopher gathered himself together, then answered softly, in a steady voice. "The first thing we need to do," he began, "is stop looking for the quick fix. That's part of the problem with American industry—looking for quick and easy solutions to complex and deeply rooted problems. A big reason the 'Japanese Way' has become so popular in this country is that it seems like a fast cure for a difficult problem. But as I've tried to explain, emulating the Japanese won't work. Why? Because we are not Japanese.

"Instead of looking to the Japanese, or to anyone else, we need to look to ourselves, to America. What I propose is a plan based on American values of self-reliance, free expression, individuality, and initiative."

Christopher reached for his chart and put it on an easel. He took a short breath, then pointed to the top of the chart.

"My first recommendation," he said, "concerns specific manufacturing procedures. Our first task is to improve production techniques—to make them more efficient. We should introduce a modified *kanban* system in our factories. If we can reduce our set-up time, we can run smaller lot sizes; and if we can run smaller lots, we can reduce our lead times and cut inventory carrying costs. The result would be better asset management and higher profits, as well as better delivery to customers. We should, in addition, fully integrate robotics in certain assembly plants. General Motors is moving in this direction with its new Saturn car, and I suggest the Covenant Corporation should do the same. Implementing these manufacturing techniques will increase our productivity."

Christopher noticed that some managers were taking notes,

while a few others looked on, apparently interested. Lagrange sat staring at the blank tablet in front of him.

"The second point in my program concerns quality control," Christopher continued. "Like many American companies, the Covenant Corporation prospered during the fifties and sixties, and stopped demanding high quality in its products. The Japanese, meanwhile, worked hard to change their image as manufacturers of low quality goods. How did they transform themselves into the most quality conscious producers in the world? Well, it wasn't because of anything innately Japanese. In fact, all of their quality control ideas came from Americans—Deming, Juran, and Cummings. In the late fifties, when these scientists were being ignored in America, they found an audience in Japan. It was by adopting the statistical quality control methods of these Americans that Japan learned to produce quality goods. And my recommendation is that we don't need to go to Japan to learn about quality—the source is right here in our backyard, if we would only look."

To emphasize the point, Christopher held up a hardcover book titled *Statistical Quality Control Handbook*. "See this?" he asked. "This book was published by Western Electric in 1956. It describes the quality control methods invented by Americans and adopted by the Japanese. I strongly recommend we institute a program using this text to train our engineers and technicians in statistical quality control—complete with $\bar{X}$ and $\bar{R}$ charts, process control charts, and the like."

"But, Newman," a manager asked, "isn't the lack of quality really the fault of our employees? We've given the employees so much—benefits, retirement, profit sharing, open door policies—that they've gotten too secure, too lazy to be productive. Don't you think we need more discipline? I think a little terror might improve our quality more quickly than using charts."

Laughter followed his remark.

"Unfortunately," Christopher responded, "the blame, though partly the workers', lies largely with management."

The room went quiet. "Now wait a minute—" the man began.

"Look," Christopher interrupted, "is somebody here going to dispute Deming's authority in these matters?"

No one answered.

"Well," Christopher continued, "when Deming was asked who was to blame for the decline in quality control in America, he said that three parties were responsible: management, management, and management. That's because the worker invariably takes the direction set by management. And if management doesn't insist on quality control, it's not going to happen."

"It's important to have high expectations of our employees," said Merriweather in a conciliatory tone, "and I agree that management has to set the example."

Christopher pushed on. "The need for high expectations leads directly to my next point. We have to insist on excellence—in both spirit and practice. Not by imposing conformity or coercion, but by combining individual initiative with overall goals through Management By Objectives, as Peter Drucker calls it. The manager sets the objectives and provides the general direction, then lets the employee use his own initiative and methods, within the larger framework of the department, to achieve the goal. As I see it, this gives us the best of both worlds—the individual can be in control of the job and responsible for his or her work; and, at the same time, the company can accomplish its goals. Workers are no longer alienated from their work. And the company benefits not only from the completed task, but also from the positive attitude the employees develop toward their jobs."

"I don't know about that, Newman," said a female executive. "MBO works among managers and line supervisors, but trying it with our blue collar workers seems risky. I think we'd really be going overboard if we tried MBO on the factory floors."

"We won't know until we try," Christopher said. "But one

thing is certain: we're not going to get anywhere using Japanese methods. Americans are just too individualistic to put up with ritualistic groupings for too long. What we want is voluntary teamwork, not coerced cooperation. We're already seeing teamwork at companies like Hewlett-Packard, and it's being accomplished without relying on Japanese methods. It's working by stressing worker participation and MBO, so that teamwork grows out of self-interest, rather than being imposed from above."

"All very idealistic," Lagrange said, shaking his head. He didn't look up as he spoke, but continued to stare at the tablet before him.

"Not at all," Christopher countered. "What I'm talking about is absolutely practical, and it has precedence in American business. Does anyone remember Robert Townsend's book *Up the Organization?*"

A few people murmured recognition of the title and nodded.

"That book offered some very practical advice on how to run a company. All of Townsend's advice was derived from his own experience, all of it was implemented, and *none* of it," Christopher emphasized, "was learned from the Japanese. And his advice really made sense. He stressed 'excellence, fun, and justice;' he advocated an unpretentious and open style of management that was concerned with fairness and quality. In short he talked about another way to arrive at the results we're now trying to get from copying the Japanese! Townsend didn't try to get us to behave like another people; he told us to be smart Americans."

Christopher paused to turn a page in his notes. "What's more," he added, "Townsend's advice is essentially the same as that given by early American writers and thinkers like Emerson and Thoreau: self-reliance, common sense, simplicity, pragmatism, and above all, don't imitate—work with the reality before you."

"Emerson? Thoreau? What the—" Lagrange sputtered. He

was turning red, and his cigarette smoke enveloped him, causing him to squint and choke.

"There is a connection, I'm sure," said Merriweather quickly. "And it could work at the Covenant Corporation. It's certainly worth thinking about, don't you agree?"

He turned to the group at large. No one responded. Several executives glowered at the Director of Personnel. "Uh, what else do you have in mind?" he asked Christopher, not without effort.

"I have two final recommendations. Both involve cooperation between business and government. After all, our government shapes the economic environment, and it plays an important part in Covenant's productivity.

"In particular, we have to press the government to lower the federal deficit. This will bring down interest rates and make it easier for American companies to invest in new equipment. As long as we face high borrowing costs, we'll have a hard time modernizing our plants and staying competitive. And lower interest rates will also help correct the present disparity in exchange rates and will make our products more attractive to foreign buyers.

"Finally, we need to work with government to overcome trade barriers. The Japanese have major obstacles to imports—some of them are explicit, and many are based on tradition and custom. But the effect is the same: American firms are denied access to Japanese markets. Our government needs to adopt a strong trade policy that gives us reciprocal access to markets around the world."

"Come on, Newman," called a man from the far side of the room. "Do you really expect the government to help us? All the government will do is interfere with our free market system."

"Not at all," Christopher countered. "President Reagan appointed a special Commission on Industrial Competitiveness, which specifically called for lower capital costs and greater emphasis on trade policy. But now we have to urge the government to follow through on these recommendations.

"Besides, we might have a free market economy, but Japan doesn't. For example, the Japanese government gives companies low-interest funds to encourage research and development. To be competitive, we need something similar, like tax incentives for investment and capital formation, and relaxation of anti-trust laws that restrict joint ventures in research and development. It's already beginning to happen. Under the National Cooperative Research Act, companies can now pool their basic research. In this case, the government had to relax its anti-trust laws or the American electronics industry could be threatened. Or consider Chrysler. Without government help, it would have folded. Instead, Chrysler's more profitable than ever, and paid the government back well ahead of schedule.

Ridgeman looked at his watch and smiled awkwardly. Lagrange simply sat, smoke billowing from him. Interest in Christopher's talk had almost vanished.

"Well, those are my recommendations," said Christopher. "If I can put my argument simply, let me say that we shouldn't fall for a naive imitation of the Japanese system—the trappings, rituals, and quaint customs are trivial. Don't fall for the approach advocated by *The Book of Five Rings*—confusing windy mysticism with hard work. Let's look to our own experience and improve what we've got. Before I went to Japan I thought I would find the 'secret,' the solution to all our problems. All I found was that the grass is rarely greener on the other side of the hill. Thank you."

There was silence, then, after a moment, a sprinkling of half-hearted applause. Ridgeman stood up and cleared his throat. "Any comments?" he asked, looking around and smiling awkwardly.

"If I understand you, Mr. Newman," said a manager at the far end of the table, "you're suggesting a broad range of things that would take quite a bit of time to implement. I think we need a quicker remedy! What are we going to do to turn the company around right now?"

"Well," Christopher answered, "as I tried to say before, there are no quick and easy solutions. The problems are complex, and they demand careful, long-term solutions."

"But we don't have time to wait!" another executive interrupted. "Come on, Newman! Didn't you find something in Japan that can solve our problems today?"

Christopher sighed. There are no immediate solutions, he thought. That's exactly what I've been trying to tell them. But nobody wants to listen; everyone wants to find a magical answer.

"I don't believe there's a single solution to our problems," Christopher began explaining in a patient tone. "We need to attack these problems in a broad way. And we can't look to the Japanese; we have to look to ourselves."

Several managers grumbled and frowned. Two men rose from their seats and began to walk out.

Lagrange stood up suddenly and jabbed his finger accusingly at Christopher.

"Newman, your inability to isolate the secret of Japanese productivity shows how weak your report is! You haven't told us a thing! We need a solution and we need it now, and you're not giving it to us! Newman, this report is a failure."

Others echoed their agreement. Christopher looked away and shook his head slowly. Why couldn't they see?

Ridgeman stood up, shaken and dejected.

"Uh, thank you all for your attendance," he said loudly, seeking to end the session as quickly as possible. "The meeting is adjourned! Let's all get back to work."

Grunting with approval, the executives gathered their papers and began filing out of the room. A few looked back at Christopher, but most left quickly and without further word. No doubt they would return to their offices and proceed with business as usual, Christopher thought. He felt totally numb.

When all but Ridgeman and Mrs. Bloom had left, the president walked up to Christopher.

"It wasn't all your fault," said Ridgeman. "I made a mistake in assigning the project to you. I guess it was just over your head."

"Did *you* think my presentation was a failure?" Christopher asked.

Ridgeman paused for a moment. "That'll be all, Newman," he said.

As Christopher gathered his papers, Ridgeman walked back to Mrs. Bloom and leaned over to talk with her.

"Mrs. Bloom," he said in a whisper loud enough for Christopher to overhear, "I want you to call Lagrange and have him meet with me at once. I'm going to send him to Japan—he'll find the secret of Japanese management without any trouble. Three days in Japan should be enough. He's got a good mind for this sort of assignment. And I can't afford to let Lynch down."

"I'll call him right away," Mrs. Bloom replied.

Christopher shuddered. Lagrange in Japan? What a joke. Lagrange didn't even know the time of day. He'd probably come back from Japan and recommend factory housing, company slogans, and relaxed safety standards. Christopher shook his head sadly, then reached for his papers and walked from the room.

Chapter 13

Christopher left the conference room and walked along the dimly lit corridor to his office. Once inside he closed the door softly and let out a deep sigh. It was a relief to be done with the meeting; it felt good to get away from the executive committee and its narrow attitudes. He looked around his office. It was calm and still, and gave him a sense of tranquillity.

Placing his papers on the large oak desk, Christopher moved over to the window and stared down from the forty-fifth floor. Morning traffic, distant and silent, streamed through the city streets. Christopher scarcely noticed. He stood quietly, hands in his coat pockets, looking off into space, his thoughts still on the meeting.

It wasn't the criticism that had bothered him most. The worst part was that they hadn't listened to him. No one, aside from Merriweather, had tried to understand him. The others had rejected his proposals out of hand, blinded by the same old prejudices and assumptions that were responsible for Covenant's predicament in the first place.

Well, he thought ruefully, I did my best. I told them what they needed to hear, but they just weren't ready for it. Maybe Covenant will decide to adopt Japanese rules and practices, and find out the hard way that some things can't be transplanted, that we have to look to ourselves for the answers. Maybe things will have to get worse before they get better.

Christopher turned and carefully surveyed the office. He studied the plush carpet, the solid oak desk with his gold name plate, the matching furniture, and the videocassette deck perched on the wall. A week earlier he had been impressed by the office and its elaborate decor. Now it meant nothing. In fact, he realized, this very office—with its luxury and trappings of power—was typical of what was wrong with the company. Management emphasized appearance rather than substance; it talked about communication but hid on the top floor of a skyscraper; it spent thousands of dollars to send him halfway around the world, but it wouldn't listen to his findings when he returned.

The office was no longer a refuge from the attitudes of the corporation—it *was* the corporation. Christopher shook his head. How could he continue to serve as Director of Corporate Productivity when he disagreed with management on such fundamental issues? Why should he stay when no one would seriously consider his recommendations? The conclusion was unavoidable. There was no longer a place for him at the Covenant Corporation. To stay on would be pointless.

Walking from the window, Christopher sat down in the visitor's chair across from the oak desk. If I leave the company, he wondered, where will I go? What will I do? He sat quietly, a multitude of thoughts and fears and ideas flooding his mind.

He thought of Emerson, whose writings counseled him to follow his heart, to scorn imitation, and never to be a "secondary man."

He thought of Mark Truitt, who had abandoned a promising career in business to become a historian.

He thought of the ice cream vendor near the university, who preferred independence to prosperity.

And he thought of Ken Yusi, who had forged his own career in the midst of an intolerant system.

At least here in America I can leave without stigma, Christopher said to himself. But where will I go? I want to stay in business, but I want to work for a company that believes in the same things I do. I'd like to have a small firm of my own, where I could establish the policies and be in charge. But what sort of firm? Suddenly he had an idea. Ken Yusi had mentioned starting an import-export company—perhaps the two of them could work as partners. The idea was attractive. They could form a small company specializing in international trade, and would follow the principles of pragmatic and open management espoused by Townsend and Drucker. Their company would involve genuine cooperation between America and Japan—it would be an equal partnership, based on real trust and respect. Christopher smiled at the irony. This trading firm, founded by a free-thinking American and a Japanese nonconformist, could be a model for cooperative business relations between their two nations.

"That's what I'll do," Christopher said aloud to himself. "I'll call Ken in the morning and propose my plan."

Taking a pad of paper from the desk, Christopher wrote out his letter of resignation. It was brief, courteous, and succinct, thanking Ridgeman and wishing him success in coming years. He signed the letter, attached his credit card and Japanese phrase book, and placed the items in his Out basket.

It was over. There was nothing left but to go home.

On his way to the lobby he passed Mrs. Bloom's desk. She looked up and smiled.

"Oh, Mr. Newman! Could I please have your credit card back? Mr. Lagrange is going to need it right away—he's leaving for Japan this afternoon."

Christopher returned her smile. "It's in my Out basket."

"Oh, thank you!" Mrs. Bloom said cheerfully.

"You're welcome," said Christopher, turning and walking on. Somehow, he felt a great sense of relief.

The elevator took him from the forty-fifth floor to street level, where he walked through the lobby and out through the skyscraper's tall glass doors. The sidewalk was busy with pedestrians and traffic sped along the avenue. Two joggers ran past. Christopher took note of them: one black man and one white man; one running with long, graceful strides, and the other taking short, quick steps; one wearing shorts and a T-shirt, the other dressed in a sweatsuit. At the corner newsstand, the vendor and a customer were arguing about politics.

A taxicab screeched to a stop and the driver yelled at a truck that had cut in front of him. In the alcove of the neighboring building, a quartet of classical musicians, apparently from the nearby conservatory, played a selection from Bach. Christopher stopped to take in the scene.

"Excuse me," someone said behind him. It was a young girl jogging by, probably before work. He watched her proceed up the street, and smiled to himself.

Looking up, Christopher saw that the early morning clouds had lifted and the day was clear and bright. He returned to his car and drove home.

For Further Reading

Of the many thick volumes about business and management, two have become standards in the field and merit special attention: Peter Drucker's *Management: Tasks, Responsibility, Practices* (Harper & Row, 1973) and George Steiner's *Strategic Planning*, (The Free Press, 1979). Both books offer extensive and thoughtful treatment of their subjects.

But what a manager often needs is a primer that can be consulted frequently for practical advice and common sense. Some especially good ones—to be kept within a manager's reach—are these: *No-Nonsense Management* (Bantam Books, 1981) by Richard S. Sloma is a pragmatic guide to management. Succinct, honest, and clearly written, it is highly recommended for managers at all levels. *Up the Organization* (Knopf, 1970) by Robert Townsend is a classic of business advice. At times glib but always stimulating, this book is irreverent and lots of fun. *The Mind of the Strategist* (McGraw-Hill, 1982) is by Kinichi Ohmae, head of McKinsey & Company's Tokyo office. Subtitled "The Art of Japanese Management," this is an excellent book on strategic thought and offers many useful lessons. It provides cases from both American and Japanese business to illustrate strategic choices and business decision-making.

Readers interested in a more detailed treatment of Japanese production management should read Richard J. Schonberger's *Japanese Manufacturing Techniques* (Free Press, 1982). This book identifies techniques that can be used in America and explores them in sufficient depth to be valuable for any production manager or engineer. There are sections on "Just-in-Time"

Production, "Total Quality Control," and the "kanban" inventory management system. The aim is to simplify the manufacturing process and make it more efficient. To learn more about quality circles and how they can be successful in an American company, refer to *Quality Circles* (Addison-Wesley, 1983) by William and Harriet Mohr. This book stresses how traditional American values are well suited to successful quality circles and can help improve quality in manufacturing.

Of the many books available on Japan and the Japanese, the best one for a general audience is Edwin Reischauer's *The Japanese*, (Harvard University Press, 1977). This book covers a wide range of topics in a scholarly yet very readable fashion, and is an excellent source of information about Japan and its people. Another fine book that deals more specifically with the relation between Japanese culture and economy, and points out shortcomings of the Japanese system, is *Shadows of the Rising Sun* (Morrow, 1983) by Jared Taylor.

For the manager interested in the cultural context of American capitalism, a good place to start is with Ralph Waldo Emerson's work. Especially useful is Stephen Whicher's anthology, *Selections from Ralph Waldo Emerson* (Houghton Mifflin, 1957). Whicher's selections are comprehensive, clearly and efficiently introduced, yet the volume is compact and handy as a reference book. It contains the pivotal essay, "Self-Reliance."

Two other major American writers, Henry James and Mark Twain, offer astute analyses of the American character that can prove useful in business situations. James's novels, particularly *The American*, depict the American innocent attempting to cope with, and in a sense emulate, an alien culture. Inevitably the Jamesian hero fails in his quest, and is thrown back upon his own resources. As a complement to James, Twain's novel *Huckleberry Finn* focuses on the resurgent strength and necessity of American individualism. In deciding to follow the dictates of his conscience rather than yield to societal pressures, Huck Finn reaffirms the American ideal of self-reliance and individualism. In its economic manifestation, this spirit of independence recurs as the entrepreneur who functions as the force of renewal in American business. Both James's and Twain's novels are widely available in a variety of imprints.

A final note: The manager or business professional can learn much from Daniel Bell's critique, *The Cultural Contradictions of Capitalism* (Basic Books, 1976), which does a good job of exposing the cultural matrix underlying modern American capitalism. His analysis is insightful and provocative, and worthy of careful consideration.

Selected Bibliography

Bruce-Briggs, B. "The Dangerous Folly Called Theory Z." *Fortune*, 17 May 1983, pp. 41–53. How cultural differences make imitating the Japanese very problematic.

Byron, Christopher. "How Japan Does It." *Time*, 30 March 1981, pp. 54–60. An uncritical view of the Japanese system, looking for the "secret."

Chira, Susan. "Against the Japanese Grain." *New York Times Magazine*, 20 June 1982, pp. 28–46. The strong pressure to conform in Japanese society.

Cummings, William K. *Education and Equality in Japan*. Princeton: Princeton University Press, 1980. A scholarly study of Japanese schools. Very informative, well researched, but tends to be uncritical.

Fukutake, Tadashi. *Japanese Society Today*. Tokyo: University of Tokyo Press, 1974. A balanced view of contemporary Japan by one of its leading sociologists.

Junkerman, John. "We Are Driven: Life on the Fast Line at Datsun," *Mother Jones*, August 1982, pp. 21–40. Oppressive conditions in Japanese factories.

Kamada, Satoshi. *Japan in the Passing Lane*. New York: Random House, 1983. First Japanese publication, 1973. A critical account of manufacturing and the life of factory workers.

Musashi, Miyamoto. *The Book of Five Rings: The Real Art of Japanese Management*. New York: Bantam Books, 1982. A useful book if you're a sixteenth-century Samurai warrior.

Obojski, Robert. *The Rise of Japanese Baseball Power*. Radnor, PA: Chilton Book Co., 1975. The history of baseball in Japan.

Ouchi, William G. *Theory Z*. New York: Avon Books, 1981. Uncritical view of Japanese management. Mentions expensive "cramming" courses for preschoolers, layoffs of women during recessions, but ignores unsavory implications.

Reischauer, Edwin O. *The Japanese*. Cambridge: Harvard University Press, 1977. Readable yet scholarly, this is an excellent book by one of our leading experts on Japan. Especially useful are chapters on the group, education, women, psychological traits, daily life and customs, language, attitudes toward the land, and mass culture.

Sayle, Murray. "The Yellow Peril and the Red-Haired Devils." *Harper's*, November 1982, pp. 23–35. How little America and Japan understand each other.

"What Can the Japanese Teach U.S. Management: What is Transferable to the West and What Is Not." *World Business Weekly*, 19 January 1981. How cultural differences limit what America can learn from Japan.

Index

Adolescents, 92–94
Americans, 61–62, 92, 105–6, 127–28
Apple (co.), 107
Auto industry, 58, 99

Baseball, 69, 71–77
Book of Five Rings, The, 13–15, 16, 119
Bullet train, 61–62
Bushido, 13–15
Business, 118–19; books about, 126–28
Business practices, ii, 64, 85–87, 105; and culture and values, 49, 112–13

Capitalism, 127, 128
Child rearing, 45, 47–48, 103
Children, 32–33, 34, 37, 38–39
China, 35, 36, 68
Chrysler (co.), 119
Commission on Industrial Competitiveness, 118–19
Company(ies), 44, 48, 66–67
Competitiveness, 118–19
Conformity, 39, 40, 48, 64, 88, 90; pressure for, 105, 112
Cooperation, 52, 91, 96, 105, 113, 124
Creativity, 39, 89, 96, 112
Culture, ii, 7, 16, 30, 38, 44–45, 48, 78, 90; and economic system, iii–iv, 49, 127; effect on business practices, 64–65, 105, 111, 112–13
Customer satisfaction, ii, 91, 111
Customs, ii, 111, 113, 119

Deming, W. E., 55–56, 99, 115, 116
Dobyns, Lloyd, 86
Drucker, Peter, 116, 124
Duty, 44, 45, 48

Economic growth, 62, 65, 87
Economy: and culture, iii–iv, 49, 127
Edison, Thomas, 40
Educational system, 27, 31–40, 45, 50, 52, 86, 91, 96, 102, 112
Efficiency, 5, 9, 20, 30, 50, 58, 59, 86, 110, 114; production, 54, 97, 99, 100
Emerson, Ralph Waldo, 89–91, 92, 94, 107, 117, 123, 127
Employment: guaranteed, 105 (*see also* Lifetime employment); leaving, 63–64, 66, 67, 112
Entrepreneurship, 28, 107–8, 123–24, 128
Environment, 61, 62

Factories, 50, 91; safety in, 98, 100–1
Family life, 43–47, 48, 91, 102
Ford, Henry, 40
Free market economy, 11–12, 118, 119
Freedom, 89, 90, 92, 96, 106–7, 113

Gender discrimination, 29–30, 46, 52, 111–12
General Motors, 114
GNP, 62, 87, 113
Government: and business, 118–19
Group (the), 48, 68, 91, 92, 96, 98, 113

Harmony, 28, 29, 30, 48, 52, 54, 63, 86, 98, 101, 105; preservation of appearance of, 68, 73, 74, 75
Hewlett-Packard, 117
History, 8, 34, 35–36
Hitachi (co.), 96
Honor/dishonor, 25, 26, 28, 38, 43, 63–64, 76, 77, 112, 113
Hotels, 19–20
Housing, 43–44, 48, 62–63, 103; company, 20, 56–57, 66, 67

IBM, 96, 107
"If Japan Can, Why Can't We?" (documentary), 6, 86
Independence, personal, 39, 45, 48, 105
Individual (the), 88, 92, 93–94, 96
Individualism, American, 127–28
Individuality, 39, 89, 90, 96, 112, 113, 114
Initiative, 114, 116
Innovation, 28, 40, 82, 96
Intel (co.), 28
Invention, 89, 96, 99, 100
Inventory management, 23, 111, 112; just-in-case method, 53; just-in-time method, 52–54, 55, 99–100, 126–27

James, Henry, 105–6, 127, 128
Japan: imitation of, ii, 7, 12, 43–44, 59, 60–61, 62, 91–92, 106, 111, 113, 114, 117, 119, 122; as model, 8, 33, 58–59, 85, 90. *See also* United States/Japan differences
Japanese business/economic success, 5, 33, 48, 67–68, 82, 86–87, 96, 113; "secret" of, 4–5, 6–7, 9, 10, 13, 14–15, 24, 25, 31, 48–49, 69, 103, 106, 110–11, 120–21
Japanese Society, 45, 65, 80, 91, 94, 99,

111, 112; failure in, 38, 39, 40; protocol of, 16, 41, 42, 64–65, 95; shame in, 75, 77, 99, 102
Japanese system: failure of, 90, 127
Juran, J. M., 56, 99, 115

Kogai (public injury), 62
Korea, 35, 36, 58, 68, 100

Labor-management relations, 25, 66–67
Lifetime employment, 27, 28–29, 46, 52, 111–12
Living National Treasures, 65
Loyalty, 34, 86; coerced, 87, 88, 105, 112; worker, 27–28, 48, 67, 98

Management, iii, 49, 50, 123; books about, 126–28; Japanese approach to, 6–7, 8, 14, 15, 60, 63, 73, 85; and quality control, 115–16; "secret" of Japanese, 6–7, 110–11, 121; style of, 117, 124
Management by Objectives (MBO), 116–17
Manufacturing management: *kanban* system of, 52–55, 57–58, 59, 90, 114
Manufacturing procedures, 114–15
Meiji Restoration, 35

National Cooperative Research Act, 119
Natural resources, 62, 100

Obedience, 96, 113
Obligation, 45. *See also* Duty
Order, 23, 30, 50, 82, 96, 107
Organization, 18–19, 20, 59, 88

Philippines, 68
Production, 85, 95; flow of, 26, 27, 101
Production management, 101–2, 126–27
Production operations, 52–56, 57–58, 63, 97–101, 114–15
Productivity, ii, 2, 5, 31, 57, 67, 87, 97–99, 110, 113, 114; secret of Japanese, 8, 21, 23, 24, 25, 27–28, 48, 69, 91, 96, 120
Protectionism, 12, 68

Quality control, 24, 52, 53, 55, 99, 127; statistical, 55–56, 115
Quality of life, 62–63, 87, 113

Reagan, Ronald, 118
Regimentation, 82, 96, 112
Repetition, 24, 73, 74, 96, 112
Research and development (R&D), 96, 97, 99–100, 119

Robotics, 25, 114
Russo-Japanese War, 35

Safety, plant, 98, 100–1
Seiko (co.), 96
Self-reliance, 90, 113, 114, 117, 127
"Self-Reliance" (Emerson), 89, 127
Sexism, 66. *See also* Gender discrimination
Shipbuilding, 58
Shockley, William, 28
Sports, 73–77, 96, 102, 112
Standard of living, 62
Statistical Quality Control Handbook, 115
Steel, 58, 100
Sumo, 68–69, 78–84

Teamwork, 55, 63, 117
Technology: and culture, 16, 30
Theory Z, 21, 86
Thoreau, Henry David, 117
Tokyo, 16–17, 19, 21, 85, 88, 105
Tokyo University, 46, 79
Trade policy, 118, 119
Twain, Mark, 105, 127–28

Uchi, 44, 45
Ueno Park (Tokyo), 79, 86, 87–88, 91–94
Unions, 25, 67
United States: answer to problems of, lies in, 84, 90–92, 106, 114–20, 122; economic success of, 33, 82; individuality and freedom in thought of, 89–91; "quick-fix" solutions, 91, 114, 120. *See also* Values, U.S.
United States/Japan differences: in baseball, 71–77; in culture and values, 48, 49, 50, 58, 60–61, 63, 82, 84, 90, 95–96, 103, 105, 111, 112–13

Values: effect on business practices, 112–13, 114; Japanese, 49, 77, 111, 113; U.S., 89, 90, 113, 114, 127

Western Electric, 115
Whicher, Stephen, 127
Women, 57; education mamas, 33–34, 37, 45, 46; employment discrimination, 29–30, 45–46, 52, 111–12; place of, 66; role of, 45–46, 48
Work pace, 26, 54–55, 57, 97–98
Workers, 5, 24, 25, 54–55, 115, 116–17; pressure on, 55, 58, 63, 66, 87, 97–98, 101–2
Working conditions, 57–58

Yanagimachi, Mitsuo, 65
Yokkaichi, 62